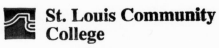

Alan Kennedy

JAPANESE COSTUME

History and Tradition

With 156 illustrations, 110 in color

KONECKY&KONECKY

Acknowledgments

It was sometime during the winter of 1988 that Sheila Hicks suggested, or rather urged, that I contact Monique Lévi-Strauss, who was serving as editor for a series of books on textiles. Thanks to Sheila's initial push, Monique's enlightened guidance, and the publishing skills of Adam Biro, this book has become a reality.

Jeffrey and Toril Hayden were the first people to open my eyes to the beauty and creativity of Japanese textiles and costumes. In the further pursuit of this subject, I am also indebted to curators and conservators at museums around the world for providing access to objects under their care. Krishnā Riboud, founder of the Association for the Study and Documentation of Asian Textiles (A.E.D.T.A.), must be thanked for her continuing encouragement and generosity.

The difficult and crucial task of securing photographs from Japanese institutions was expertly performed by Noriko Tomita. Margot Paul Ernst, with her long experience in editing books on Japanese art, provided helpful suggestions in regard to the text. Dianne Cullinane at Éditions Adam Biro did an excellent job of editing the manuscript and being the transatlantic liaison between myself and the publishing house.

Lastly, I am further indebted to Sheila Hicks for her wise counsel at every stage of the project.

Pages 2-3 :
A traditional horse race along the banks of the Kamo River in Kyoto is vividly rendered in this *yūzen kosode*. The colored maple leaves are a sign of autumn.
Another consequence of the wider *obi* was the appearance of *kosode* designs that differed significantly from top to bottom. An abstract checkered pattern contrasts strikingly with the realistic scene below.
First half of the 18th century.
1989. Kyoto National Museum, All rights reserved.

Author's Notes to the Text and Captions

1. Japanese names are given in the traditional manner, with family names first.
2. The usual names for Japanese historical periods, such as Momoyama and Edo periods, are not used because of a lack of consensus on the dates which mark those periods. Time periods which will be used are *nengō* (Japanese era names) and centuries.
3. Japanese terms which have entered Western languages through common usage will not be italicized. Those which have not will be italicized and will not be used in plural form, in keeping with Japanese language rules.
4. The text will not contain specific references to illustrations ; however, the captions will be as detailed as possible.
5. All the costumes illustrated use silk as the primary textile fiber, unless otherwise noted.
6. Measurements of costumes are not given in the captions, since they tended to be standardized in Japanese garments. For *kosode* and most *shōzoku*, dimensions range from approximately 120 to 155 cm in width (measured across the top of the shoulders from sleeve end to sleeve end) and 130 to 160 cm in height (as measured from shoulder to hem, not including the collar). *Kesa* average from 150 to 215 cm in width and from 90 to 125 cm in height.

See drawings page 6
A front view of the garment which is assembled from the seven pieces of cloth obtained from the cutting layout shown below.
An illustration (not drawn to scale) of the component parts of the *kosode* as derived from a single, narrow length of cloth. This same layout is applicable for several kinds of Nō theater costumes.
Dotted lines indicate the top of the garment, at which point the sleeves and body panels are folded, becoming the front and back of the robe. In designing the garment, motifs must be reserved at the fold lines in order to appear upright on both the front and back of the finished costume. Care must also be taken to assure that motifs are aligned across seams.
Adapted from Eiko Kamiya, ed., « Kosode, » *Nihon no bijitsu*, vol. 67, 1971, pp. 33-34.

Printed in Italy

Series Editor: Monique Lévi-Strauss

Contents

Introduction

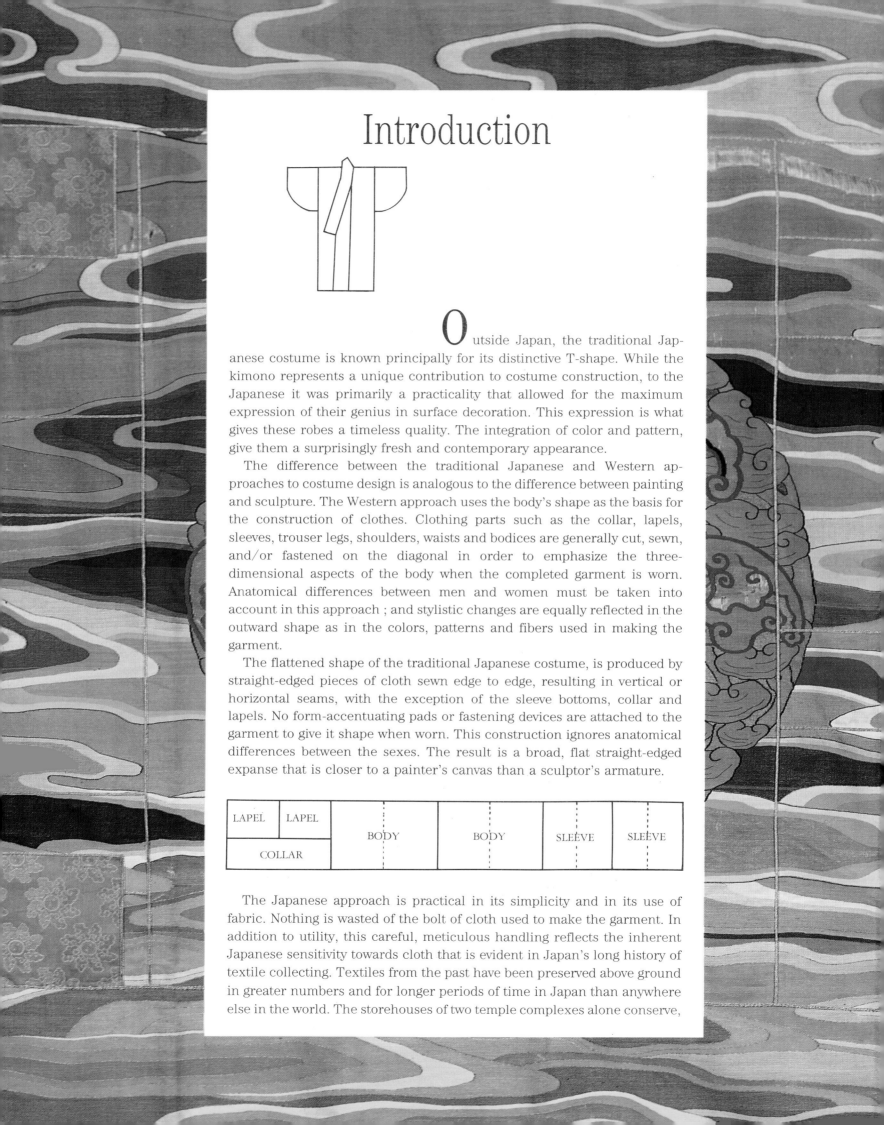

Outside Japan, the traditional Japanese costume is known principally for its distinctive T-shape. While the kimono represents a unique contribution to costume construction, to the Japanese it was primarily a practicality that allowed for the maximum expression of their genius in surface decoration. This expression is what gives these robes a timeless quality. The integration of color and pattern, give them a surprisingly fresh and contemporary appearance.

The difference between the traditional Japanese and Western approaches to costume design is analogous to the difference between painting and sculpture. The Western approach uses the body's shape as the basis for the construction of clothes. Clothing parts such as the collar, lapels, sleeves, trouser legs, shoulders, waists and bodices are generally cut, sewn, and/or fastened on the diagonal in order to emphasize the three-dimensional aspects of the body when the completed garment is worn. Anatomical differences between men and women must be taken into account in this approach ; and stylistic changes are equally reflected in the outward shape as in the colors, patterns and fibers used in making the garment.

The flattened shape of the traditional Japanese costume, is produced by straight-edged pieces of cloth sewn edge to edge, resulting in vertical or horizontal seams, with the exception of the sleeve bottoms, collar and lapels. No form-accentuating pads or fastening devices are attached to the garment to give it shape when worn. This construction ignores anatomical differences between the sexes. The result is a broad, flat straight-edged expanse that is closer to a painter's canvas than a sculptor's armature.

LAPEL	LAPEL	BODY	BODY	SLEEVE	SLEEVE
	COLLAR				

The Japanese approach is practical in its simplicity and in its use of fabric. Nothing is wasted of the bolt of cloth used to make the garment. In addition to utility, this careful, meticulous handling reflects the inherent Japanese sensitivity towards cloth that is evident in Japan's long history of textile collecting. Textiles from the past have been preserved above ground in greater numbers and for longer periods of time in Japan than anywhere else in the world. The storehouses of two temple complexes alone conserve,

almost 180,000 seventh and eighth century textiles.[1] Many of these textiles are foreign in origin, as is true of a large percentage of holdings in other Japanese collections.

Textiles have always played important roles in Japanese culture and ceremonies. Japanese literature from all historic periods abounds in detailed references to cloth and clothing. Fabric and costume have been and continue to be vital in traditional events such as the tea ceremony, Buddhist and Shinto rites, weddings and theatrical performances, as well as in everyday life.

Another aspect of the reverential attitude towards cloth stemmed from the traditional Japanese feeling for natural materials. Shinto, the native religion, stresses the sacredness of nature and its products. The use of such materials for artistic endeavors was not subject to the Western bias against what might be considered craft materials. A Japanese artist would have had no inhibitions about using costume as a means of expression. And, furthermore, a Japanese artist who designed cloth for costumes would have had at his disposal a wide variety of specialists in dyeing, embroidery, and weaving who were ready to execute his ideas.

Given these important pre-conditions – a perfect format for decoration, a society with a high regard for textiles, and artists unfettered by any bias against working in the textile medium – it was then only a matter of time before an environment existed in which the flowering of Japanese costume could take place. By the middle of the sixteenth century, Japan was headed towards peace and prosperity, the old social order was changing, a new spirit was in the air, and traditional sex roles were in flux. At the same time, the textile industry was making advances based on innovations from abroad and artists were ready to assimilate and adapt centuries of foreign influence in a country that would be isolated from the rest of the world in the following century. The golden age of costume lasted until the middle of the nineteenth century when Japan abandoned its policy of isolation and embarked on a course of rapid westernization.

The examples of costume that have been selected as illustrations in this book are drawn from three spheres of Japanese life : the ruling classes, the theater and Buddhism. More specifically, they include *kosode* (the forerunners of modern-day kimono) of the very wealthy and/or highly placed ; *shōzoku* (theater costumes) of the elite Nō theater actors, and *kesa* (mantles) of the high-ranking Buddhist clergy. On the whole, the clothing of these three groups was more highly valued than those of other groups, and best reflected the dynamic forces at work during this period. Consequently, they have been well cared for and carefully preserved, although subject to much wear, alteration and repair during their active lifetimes. The organization of Japanese costume into three groups will show both the similarities and differences among garments made and used for secular, theatrical and sacred purposes.

NOTES

1. These textiles are housed in the Shōsō-in, which is part of the Tōdai-ji (ji means temple) in Nara, the Hōryū-ji, located outside Nara, and the Tokyo National Museum with holdings that were formerly in the Hōryū-ji.

Military
and Political
Unification
and Rule

Pages 8-9 :
Details from an early 17th century screen painting showing a cross-section of life in Edo (modern day Tokyo), the largest city in the world by the middle of the 18th century. The men, women and children depicted include samurai, townspeople, Buddhist clerics and servants. Colorful and boldly patterned dress is worn by both men and women. The two Buddhist clerics, who are shown in black hats, are wearing a simple everyday type of *kesa* draped over their robes. On special occasions, they would wear *kesa* that were as vivid and bright-hued as the garments worn by the general population.
Collection of Idemitsu Museum of Arts, Tokyo.

J apan entered the sixteenth century in the midst of the period known as *sengoku* (country at war). Factions in the civil war included the samurai (military class), the Buddhist clergy and the court aristocracy. Power struggles took place throughout the country, within and between these groups. By mid-century, another potential rival for power appeared with the entrance of the first Europeans in Japan, led by the Portuguese who came in 1543.

Two pages from a women's encyclopedia illustrating women from all levels of society. Starting from the upper right corner and moving clockwise are a townswoman, two samurai, two farm women, two courtesans, two widows, a common prostitute, a concubine and a court lady.
10 × 6 ¾ in. (25.4 × 17.3 cm).
Published in 1847, but based on an earlier version first printed in 1692.
Illustrations by Katsushika Ōi.
Robert Ravicz Collection.

In the second half of the century, three great leaders emerged out of the chaos to centralize power and insure a peace that lasted well into the nineteenth century. Oda Nobunaga (1543-82) understood the advantage of European firearms in warfare and used them with great success in his campaigns. By 1568, he controlled Kyoto, seat of the Imperial court and of the hereditary military chief, the shogun. Nobunaga embraced Christianity, in part to counter the power of the Buddhist sects, many of whose temple strongholds and armies he destroyed.

Toyotomi Hideyoshi (1536-98) rose from humble origins through the ranks of Nobunaga's army, and succeeded him upon his assassination in 1582. Hideyoshi continued the unification of Japan, but his successor was defeated in 1600 at the battle of Sekigahara.

The third great leader, Tokugawa Ieyasu (1542-1616) declared himself shogun in 1603 and defeated Hideyoshi's remaining armies in 1615 at the battle of Osaka. Ieyasu moved the seat of the shogunate from Kyoto to Edo (modern day Tokyo), where he and his descendants were the supreme temporal rulers of a unified Japan for over 250 years. The powerless Emperor and his court remained in Kyoto.

The Tokugawas cemented their rule through a series of strong measures. Any possible foreign threats to their power were dealt with by the policy of *sakoku* (isolation of the country) and by the outlawing of Christianity. The only foreigners permitted to trade with Japan were the Dutch and Chinese, whose merchants were confined to an artificial island built in the harbor of Nagasaki. Japanese were not allowed to travel abroad. Christian converts were persecuted and many who refused to renounce Christianity were killed.

Confucianism provided the Tokugawas with a philosophy to guide them in the control of their subjects. The appeal of this ancient Chinese philosophy lay in its stress on hierarchy, duty and obedience. Social classes were ranked by importance in the following order – samurai, farmer, artisan and merchant. Buddhist clergy were not included in this hierarchy, but were individually ranked by the shogunate within their sects. The daimyo, or regional leaders of the samurai class, were assigned their domains largely on the basis of their loyalty to the Tokugawas during the civil war. To guarantee their obedience, the policy of *sankin-kōtai* was instituted, requiring them to spend alternate years in Edo, where their wives and children were forced to reside permanently. Laws set by the shogunate in Edo served as models for the daimyo in ruling their domains. Even marriages of the daimyo were subject to shogunate approval.

The ranking of classes was a useful means of social control for it took into account the changes that had taken place in society. Many merchants and artisans (known collectively as *chōnin*, literally "townspeople") had become wealthy during the unification. However, their position at the bottom of the social scale left them powerless in many ways. For instance, debts owed to them by the samurai could be cancelled by the shogunate. Farmers, who were relatively high in status, were themselves subject to oppressive demands by the samurai, whose main source of income was the rice cultivated by the farmers.

Sumptuary laws were another instrument of control used by the shogunate. *Chōnin* were most often the target of these frequently enacted laws, which regulated public displays of wealth including houses, weddings and entertainment. Clothing, the most popular form of conspicuous consumption, was often mentioned in these edicts. An account of the breaking of such a law and the severe punishment that followed is

contained in *Chōnin kōkenroku* (*A Record of Observations on Merchants and Artisans*), written circa 1728, describing an event that took place almost fifty years earlier. "There was a *chōnin* called Ishikawa Rokubei of Obune-chō in Edo... His wife was an extraordinarily ostentatious person and she went to the limit in finery. Finally they were caught in heaven's net. Along the route that the Military Lord Jōken'in took on his first visit to Ueno as shogun, Rokubei's wife and her servants, beautifully dressed, were among the spectators. The Military Lord thought that she was the wife of a daimyo or some high-ranking family. He graciously had an aide make inquiries and he was told that she was the wife of the fellow in question. After his return to the Castle, he had Rokubei and his wife summoned to the office of the town magistrate. The shogun considered outrageous their ostentatiousness beyond their station and their lack of reverence for their superiors. He confiscated their property, and although punishment should have been more severe, thanks to his gracious clemency, they received [merely] banishment from Edo."[1]

The Tokugawas astutely realized that the samurai, having no wars to fight, and the *chōnin*, having money but no status, needed outlets for their frustations. Pleasure quarters and public theaters, although subject to

Left :
This scene is one of several on a pair of painted screens depicting life in the brothel district of Kyoto. The caged courtesans are shown playing music, reading and talking with prospective customers. In the foreground, a samurai brazenly embraces a prostitute.
Each screen 49 × 150 in.
(124.5 × 380 cm).
First half of the 17th century.
Collection of Honolulu Academy of Arts, Gift of Mrs. L. Drew Betz.

Right :
Detail from an eight-panel screen painting showing busy urban life in and around a shop selling *kosode*. Customers are examining bolts of cloth and finished garments.
Each panel 24 ¼ × 16 ½ in.
(61.7 × 41.8 cm).
Mid 16th century.
Tokyo National Museum.

government regulation, were allowed to proliferate in urban areas. Courtesans and entertainers (with the exception of Nō theater actors, who had samurai status) remained outside the social hierarchy as permanent residents of an invented fantasy world.

PROSPERITY

As Japan moved from a state of civil war to unification, the economy experienced strong growth. Foreign trade had been conducted for some time with China, but it picked up considerably with the arrival of the Europeans in the sixteenth century. Business practices learned from foreigners contributed to the economic vitality of Japan. Agricultural productivity increased with improvements in irrigation and land reclamation, and was further spurred by the granting of some degree of independence to farmers along with guarantees of their safety under the protection of the emerging leaders. As the result of political stability, transportation within the country also improved, leading to the acceleration of commercial and agricultural activity.

Merchants, in particular, had benefited during the civil wars as money-lenders and intermediaries in the affairs of warring daimyo. As the country became united, a monetary economy was introduced to replace rice which, apart from being the major food staple, was also the principal unit of exchange. The shogunate assumed the exclusive right to mint coins, which greatly simplified commerce. However, the daimyo and their samurai dependents still had a rice-based income that was allocated by the shogunate. Merchants acted as brokers, using currency in the buying and selling of rice at exchange rates that they set. Taxes were still based on rice production, much to the detriment of farmers and samurai, while merchants and artisans were consequently virtually untaxed. As government spending increased with the advent of unification, inflation developed, again hurting farmers and samurai, while benefiting the *chōnin*. Merchants controlled the prices of their social superior's rice, and artisans were able to raise prices for their goods. The townspeople were thus able to protect themselves from inflation while farmers and samurai had no such recourse.

An example of the fortunes that were amassed is provided by the novelist Ihara Saikaku's (1642-93) description of the possessions of an Osaka rice merchant named Yodoya. Some of the many valuables that he is reputed to have owned included 540 buildings, 729,000 pounds of gold and silver, and 17,000 bolts of expensive cloth. The sumptuary laws passed by the government were meant to check such wealth, but, perhaps more important-ly, served to help regulate the economy during occasional periods of hardship that were brought on by famine, fire and inflation.

Rapid urbanization took place during this period of political stability and economic growth. Edo, a small fishing village in the sixteenth century, grew quickly as the seat of the shogunate and became a major commercial center. By the middle of the eighteenth century, it was the largest city in the world, with a population of over one million people. By comparison, the

(Detail)
An upper-class woman (third figure from the left) is surrounded by her entourage. Her outer robe is worn wrapped around her waist and off her shoulders in the samurai manner. The woman is accompanied by her stylishly dressed maids.
Both women and men of the samurai class found themselves attracted to the brash, modern ways of their social inferiors.
39 ⅜ × 105 ⅞ in.
(100 × 269 cm).
First half of the 17th century.
Collection of The Brooklyn Museum, Gift of Mrs. Frederic B. Pratt.

population of London and Paris were only 800,000 and 500,000 respectively. Osaka and the Kyoto were the next largest cities in Japan. In addition to those major cities, each of the fiefs apportioned to the daimyo had a central castle town that was a smaller version of the big cities.

SOCIAL INTERACTION

Although a strict social hierarchy existed by law, in actual practice there was a degree of social mobility and mixing of the classes. One common ground for class interaction was the tea ceremony. Diaries that recorded attendance at tea gatherings include merchants among the usual samurai, clerics and aristocratic guests. These merchants had probably used their wealth to establish contacts in high places and earned reputations for refined taste, a certain style or a special talent. A less elevated meeting ground was the pleasure quarter. Samurai were expected to be formal and dignified and to uphold the classical traditions of their warrior ancestors. However, it was hard to resist the fascinating world of the licensed districts, where they rubbed elbows with the largely *chōnin* clientele. There, status was attained by money and wit.

Ihara Saikaku, the novelist, wrote of illicit love affairs between members of different classes. The stories, often based on actual incidents, usually had tragic endings, since such love was in violation of the law. However, using money as a lever, a *chōnin* might be able to marry into a lower-rank samurai family, or be adopted by one that lacked a male heir. Conversely, a low-ranking samurai, with no hope of becoming rich might choose to renounce his own class and become a merchant, or, if talented, a writer or an artist. A samurai woman might be sold to a brothel by her impoverished family or banished there as punishment for a lapse of virtue. In the latter case, it was sometimes possible to enter a Buddhist monastery as an alternative to the brothel.

Hierarchy was the rule within and between social classes although one's status could change through luck, ability or persistence. Ranking was common within the four classes, and among Buddhists, the court aristocracy, and even courtesans. Courtesans were ranked according to their social origin, beauty, skill in entertaining, and conversational ability. *Ōiran* was the general term for those at the top of their profession, while common prostitutes such as *yuna*, who were hired by public bathhouses and did little in the way of entertaining, were at the bottom.

Clothing was one means by which differences in rank were reflected. A late eighteenth century novelist Shōzan, wrote of a high-ranking courtesan : "While her ravishing beauty is such that the mere sight of her face will steal away one's very soul, the gorgeousness of her wearing apparel almost defies description."[2] Distinctions in rank even extended to the quality and types of textiles used by courtesans for their bedding.

Saikaku, while sympathetic to the inherent unfairness of social hierarchy, expressed disapproval of those who did not dress according to their social status.
"In everything people have a liking for finery above their station. Women's clothes in particular go to extremes. Because they forget their proper place, extravagant women should be in fear of divine punishment... It is distressing to see a merchant wearing good silks. Pongee suits him better and looks better on him. But fine clothes are essential to a samurai's status, and therefore even a samurai who is without attendants should not dress like an ordinary person."[3]

A late 17th century painted handscroll depicting well-known *ōiran* (elite courtesans), thought to be from the licensed district of Kyoto. The three shown in this detail are individualized by their fine *kosode*, rather than their faces, which is an indication of the importance of clothing in Japanese society. Medieval poetry is written above and around the demurely posed courtesans, creating a mood of upper-class refinement. This was intended to make them even more appealing to the largely lower-class clientele who were the mainstay of the brothel business.
Complete handscroll
10 ³⁄₈ × 36 in. (26.2 × 91.7 cm).
Spencer Collection, The New York Public Library. Astor, Lenox and Tilden Foundations.

THE SPIRIT OF THE TIMES

The changing political, economic and social orders created an exhilarating atmosphere in Japan. The three great leaders, Oda Nobunaga, Toyotomi Hideyoshi and Tokugawa Ieyasu all built magnificent, lavishly decorated castles in celebration of their triumphs. Nobunaga's castle at Azuchi in Kyoto had many rooms adorned with wall paintings and painted partitions. In contrast to the monochromatic ink of traditional paintings, these works were characterized by their bold subjects and the use of gold leaf and bright colors. Hideyoshi organized several pageants, including the Grand Kitano Tea Ceremony in 1587, a five-day party to which the entire population of Kyoto was invited. One of his residences contained a tea room with walls entirely covered in gold leaf. Ieyasu was less profligate in his spending than his predecessors. Even so, he maintained a very large wardrobe. Upon his death his estate contained over 3,000 robes.[4]

The great leaders had shown the heights to which an individual could rise and the lack of restraint with which one's success could be enjoyed. The old standards of behavior set by the upper classes of the past were no longer so important to the newly powerful and their followers. The *Keichō kenbunki* of 1614 provides an account of this attitude as it related to dress, "Not only the great warlords of today but warriors of every class are concerned with beauty, wearing colorfully woven and embroidered fine silks. The warriors also decorate themselves according to their status, carefully making up their appearance, and spending all their pay on clothing."[5]

For *chōnin* money became an obsession. Saikaku wrote : "the geneologies of townspeople are written in terms of money".[6] Many of the *nouveau riche* spent money as fast as they could make it. Of Edo

merchants, it was said that they never held onto money "upon which the sun had set".[7] The new money was often spent on conspicuous items such as expensive clothing.

Money, to an extent, could even buy culture, and public performances of Nō theater were the result of a need for money. Nō troupes had been exclusively supported by, and performed for, the samurai class since the fourteenth century. When financial support from the samurai was deficient, the shogunate granted troupes the right to perform to paying public audiences in order to raise funds. It is difficult to imagine the sublimity of the Nō theater being appreciated by an audience under the conditions described in 1848 : "The tumult inside the theater was indescribable. Everyone was making so much noise all at once that it was impossible to understand what was being said."[8]

Evasion of sumptuary laws was also a part of the new materialism. The laws reflected this by the frequency with which they were reissued. The government was at least realistic about the difficulty of legislating restraint, as seen in the following law of 1686 :
"Embroidery has been prohibited in women's clothing. Its use has become common, however, and hereafter embroidered robes may be bought and sold if they are not especially sumptuous. Magnificent embroidery should not be made."[9]

Evasion ran the gamut from blatant flaunting of the rules (as in the case of Ishikawa Rokubei's wife) to subtle maneuvers such as sewing an expensive lining into a garment. Another form of evasion, used by clothing merchants, involved deceptive accounting procedures, as evidenced by this law of 1713, "for a number of years women's clothing has been sumptuous. Moreover, the price of woven material and thread imported through Nagasaki, and the cost of embroidering, dapple tie-dyeing and the like has increased, and prices have become unbelievably high. As this is improper, prohibitions were issued. In order to keep within the prescribed [maximum] price, some [merchants] declare only the cost of the gold thread [for embroidery], or the gold leaf appliqué, or the dapple tie-dyeing, or the like, having provided separately the actual material of the robe ; some combine the cost or two or three padded robes as if it were the price of one."[10]

Saikaku may even have adopted his moralizing tone in this spirit of evasion. Since his favorite subject was illicit love, he ran the risk of severe punishment for writing about such taboos. However, he was careful to criticize his protagonists as he titiliated readers with his amorous stories. It is not surprising that he was the most popular novelist of his time.

Ukiyo is the often-used term that characterizes these times. It is usually defined as the 'floating world,' referring to hedonistic life in the licensed

Above, Pages 18-19 :
The samurai women in this detail from a 17th century screen painting are engaged in the game of shuttlecock, traditionally played as part of New Year's festivities. In spite of their dignified social status, they could not resist the urge to wear sumptuous *kosode*.
Full screen 41 × 112 in. (104.2 × 284.7 cm).
Miani Johnson Collection.

Illustration of an outdoor party scene from Ihara Saikaku's novel, *Five Women Who Loved Love* (1686). A *kosode* is conspicuously draped over the cloth enclosure as a means of impressing others in the vicinity. However, the onlooker shown here is only interested in watching the dancing girls.
10 ¼ × 6 ¾ in. (26 × 17 cm).
Spencer Collection, The New York Public Library. Astor, Lenox and Tilden Foundations.

districts, but it also carried with it the connotations of being modern, fashionable and living for the moment. Originally, a similar word was used by Buddhists to convey the fleeting nature of human existence. Implicit in that definition was the importance of spirituality and other-worldliness. The way in which the meaning of *ukiyo* was inverted illustrates the practical, 'here and now' attitude that was prevalent.

This attitude hardly failed to infect Buddhists themselves. Genre paintings show Buddhist clerics participating with the rest of society in life's pleasures. Saikaku, the astute observer of his society, described a widow following the common practice of entering a Buddhist nunnery upon the death of her husband : "Among the things she must leave behind is a gown with fawn-spot designs and beautiful embroidery. 'I shall not need this any more. It should be made into a canopy or an altarcloth or a temple pennant.' But in her heart the lady is thinking : 'Too bad these sleeves are just a little too small. I might still wear them'."[11]

Materialism and conspicuous consumption inevitably led to competition at all levels of society. Stories of fashion contests, which are retold as legends, abound in the literature on Japanese costume. Wives of merchants attempted to outdo each other, sometimes in very subtle ways. The famous artist Ogata Kōrin (1658-1716) was reputedly hired to advise a rich merchant's wife for such a competition. He dressed her in an entirely black robe, making her elaborately dressed competitors look garish by comparison. Kōrin is also credited with another legendary feat of one-upmanship in the following story : "Kōrin and some of his wealthy plebeian patrons, picnicking on the banks of the Kano above Kyoto, tossed their bamboo-sheaf dumpling wrappers down-stream. A party of aristocrats lunching below caught up the leaves as they drifted past and discovered that the inside of each one had been painted with incredibly small gold lacquer designs by the master himself."[12]

A more common form of competition took place during the flower viewing festivals which were held as grandiose picnics. Ropes were strung around a group's private area, and their outer robes were then flung over the ropes, creating both a curtained enclosure and providing a convenient way of showing off their fine clothing. Saikaku described this practice : "Secluded within an enclosure formed by bright robes hanging between the trees, the daimyo's ladies, with elegant songs embroidered on their kimonos, might well be judged a sight more attractive even than the cherry blossoms themselves."[13]

Clothing competition also manifested itself in the costumes made for the Nō theater. Daimyo vied with each other in the quality and sumptuousness of the costumes that they provided for their troupes of actors, and were able to do so as these costumes were exempt from the sumptuary laws.

The *kosode* worn by these women, who are most likely courtesans, compete with their activities as the main subject of this early 18th century painted handscroll. They are shown practicing the traditional "four accomplishments" of Chinese gentlemen-scholars of the past – painting, writing poetry, playing music and board games. Their classical pursuits and fine clothing helped create an aura of refinement and beauty that especially appealed to townsmen, for whom women of the upper class were off limits. **Complete scroll 12 ³⁄₈ × 96 in. (31.5 × 243.8 cm).**

The women on the left side of the print diptych stare at the elegant courtesan in the print on the right. There are two women and a man in her retinue. She wears a broad sash (*obi*) over a plain *kosode* with fan-shaped crests showing on the shoulders. Her sense of *iki* (chic) is conveyed in the understatement of her robe and the prominence of her *obi*. Her simple *kosode* shows that she is in the vanguard of the reaction against opulent dress that began in the latter of the 18th century. A subtle moment has been captured here, as the stares of envious onlookers go coolly unacknowledged by the courtesan.
Each print 14 ¾ × 10 in. (37.5 × 25.3 cm). By Torii Kiyonaga (1752-1815).
Collection of Yale University Art Gallery, Frances Gaylord Smith Collection.

Sumptuary laws as applied to the samurai class were actually a blessing in disguise, since they provided an excuse for abstaining from this expensive competition.

In many respects the real trendsetters of society were the courtesans and entertainers of the 'floating world'. Many new styles were started there. Courtesans had to dress creatively in order to attract and impress customers, and sumptuary law enforcement was especially lax in their case. Their numbers were such (by the eighteenth century, 3,000 were registered in the Yoshiwara district of Edo) that their influence was formidable. The publishing industry, which was flourishing by the end of the seventeeth century, was responsible for the wide dissemination of new trends.

Below, pages 22-23 :
A fashion plate showing a leading courtesan from the Yoshiwara licensed district in Edo with her two attendants. New modes in dress were disseminated through these highly popular woodblock prints.
14 ½ × 10 ½ in. (36.7 ×26.7 cm).
By Isoda Koryūsai (worked C. 1760-80).
The University of Michigan Museum of Art, 1960/1.145.

Courtesans' dress and hairstyles were featured in many illustrated books and fashion plates that were widely circulated and eagerly copied.

Kabuki had a relatively late beginning as a theater form in Japan. By the time it was fully developed in the middle of the seventeenth century, Kabuki had large audiences of mostly townspeople. Kabuki actors, as well as other entertainers, were also trendsetters and popular subjects of the print medium. Stage costumes, exempt from sumptuary laws, could provide vicarious indulgence in the extravagance of dress that was otherwise proscribed. An original pattern or color worn by a popular actor often quickly found its way into public dress, and might even be named after the actor himself.

Naturally, tastes changed over time and were not necessarily determined by social class. A *chōnin* aspiring to the samurai level would be obliged to have a familiarity with classical Chinese and Japanese poetry, Nō theater and Confucian philosophy. Just as in the past, samurai who rose to power were expected to acquire the cultural accoutrements of the aristocracy. And yet samurai could not help but want to stay abreast of the latest trends coming from the 'floating world' and eagerly followed by the townspeople. The desire to be *iki*, or chic, affected even those within the shogun's castle and the Imperial palace. Sketches of garments made for Tōfukumon-in, daughter of the shogun and a consort of the Emperor, followed current fashions. Geisha, who formed a new class of courtesan beginning in the middle of the eighteenth century, were able to elevate themselves within the brothel hierarchy by sensing a change in taste. With their more simplified and subtle clothing, they became *iki* as reaction set in against the elaborate dress that had been in fashion.

SEX ROLES

Attitudes concerning male and female behavior underwent changes during the sixteenth century that continued to a lesser degree throughout the Tokugawa rule. These modifications were occasionally reflected in the resemblance between men's and women's clothing. João Rodrigues, a Portuguese interpreter who was in Japan from 1576 to 1612 remarked, "Both men's and women's robes are of the same style and fashion."[14] This was true even of the clothing worn by the great leaders, as seen in the bright colors and neutral imagery of surviving examples. Genre paintings of the time also show unisex dressing to have been common. Earlier in the century such outlandishness in men's dress would have been unlikely in public.

In keeping with this tendency, some women were know to dress in traditional male attire. Okuni, a shrine priestess, became famous late in the sixteenth century for her provocative dancing, which led to the formation of Kabuki theater in the seventeenth century. She sometimes wore the swords and clothing of a samurai and inspired many imitators. The Tokugawa government considered this outrageous female behavior to be a threat to society and banned women from the Kabuki stage in 1629. Young men (*wakashu*) then performed all male and female roles. Apparently, their licentious off-stage conduct caused them to be outlawed in the 1650's.

The young male dancer shown in this painting was known as a *wakashu*. Their reputation as prostitutes led to the prohibition of their public Kabuki performances.
By Tosa Mitusada (1738-1806).
Asian Art Museum of San Francisco
The Avery Brundage Collection 1988.48

Kabuki actor Sodezaki Miwano, an *onnagata*, specialized in female roles. He wears a striking *kosode* decorated with an outdoor scene of streams, mountains and pine trees.
12 ½ × 6 in. (31.7 × 15.2 cm).
Woodblock print by Okumura Toshinobu (active 1717-50).
Collection of The Newark Museum.

Thereafter, as in the Nō theater, older men played all of the roles. The male actors who performed the female Kabuki roles were called *onnagata*, as is still true today. As *onnagata* they became fashion trendsetters, influencing public dress.

Men's clothing became more conservative under Tokugawa rule and by the late seventeenth century was no longer interchangeable with female dress. As part of the Tokugawa policy of providing an escape valve for society, sexual expression was tolerated within the confines of the 'floating world'. In the licensed districts, male and female prostitutes provided men with a full range of sexual opportunities. There even existed a type of female prostitute who dressed as boys in order to attract Buddhist monks, who tended to be homosexual in their orientation.

For women under Tokugawa rule, such freedom of expression did not exist; in fact, their lives were highly restricted. Courtesans were usually indentured to brothels as young girls and their earnings were kept by the brothel owners and applied against money given to the families that sold or banished them into prostitution. They were not permitted to leave the licensed districts, except for special occasions. A woman of the samurai class was treated according to the Confucian belief which held that she was inferior to a man and her duty was to serve three masters, her father, husband and son. Women of the *chōnin* class fared slightly better in that Confucianism was less of a guiding principle for the lower classes. In fact, Saikaku's *chōnin* heroines are often presented as bold and daring characters in his novels.

ARTISTIC ACTIVITY

The wide-ranging changes in Japanese life that were set into motion during the sixteenth century had a very positive effect on artistic activity. Peace, prosperity, a new class of patrons and an infectious *joie de vivre* created ideal conditions for artistic expression. Those forces, in combination with the basic Japanese aesthetic, resulted in one of the most fertile periods in Japanese art.

One element of the Japanese aesthetic that came to light during this time was the fascination with things foreign and the readiness to copy and then assimilate new outside influences. This has been a tendency throughout Japan's history and is still strong to this day. In regard to dress, court costume had for a long time followed Chinese models, and continued to do

Nishikawa Sukenobu (1671-1750), a well-known print-maker, also designed *kosode*. This double page at the beginning of a book on *kosode* designs shows the artist being advised by the woman on his right as he sketches a design.
8 ⅝ × 11 ⅜ in. (22 × 29 cm).
Nishikawa hiinagata (1718).

Dress was often emphasized in genre painting, and was occasionally the sole subject of a screen painting. Screens such as this one are called *tagasode* (literally " whose sleeves ") because clothing draped over a rack provoked curiosity as to the identity of the owners of such fashionable *kosode*.
Photo courtesy of Eskanazi, Milan.
Private collection.

Page 28 :
A page from an album of one hundred dyed silk swatches used as color samples for *kosode*. Natural dyes made of vegetal matter were formulated and applied in secret, complicated methods that were passed down through generations of dyers. Synthetic dyes were introduced into Japan during the mid-19th century, leading to the decline of the natural dye industry.
Color names were constantly being invented. They were often poetic, such as " red dew, " the name for the top swatch ; or were based on natural phenomena, such as " summer leaf, " the name for the green swatch. Names of colors were also chosen in order to circumvent sumptuary laws which forbade the use of certain colors by particular social classes. Colors were also named in honor of popular figures, for example, *Kabuki* actors, who were identified with a particular color that appeared on one of their stage costumes.
6 × 8½ in. (15.4 × 21.4 cm).
Private collection

so. European clothing also made an impact, as can be seen from this Portuguese missionary's report in 1594, "[Hideyoshi] has become so enamoured of Portuguese dress and costume that he and his retainers frequently wear this apparel, as do all the other Lords of Japan."[15]

This influence proved to be short-lived, ending with the reaction against Europeans that came with *sakoku* (isolation of the country). Some motifs of European origin, such as the lily and the dandelion, continued to be present in Japanese costume design, as did certain articles of European dress, such as the rain cape called *kappa* (based on the Portuguese word for this garment). Another European import that had a continued use in Japanese costume was woollen cloth, known by the name *rasha* (also based on a Portuguese word).

Chinese culture had always been the strongest outside influence on Japanese life, and continued to be so, but to a lesser degree than ever before. The majority of motifs in Japanese art were Chinese in origin, but they were altered in scale, color and/or composition and Japanicized in the process. With *sakoku* came the opportunity to assimilate fully centuries of past borrowings in an environment that was relatively free of new outside input. Some of the Japanese tendencies in the art of the period included asymmetry, discontinuity, inverse proportion and bold coloration, which acted upon a range of motifs taken from geometry, nature, everyday life and the legendary past.

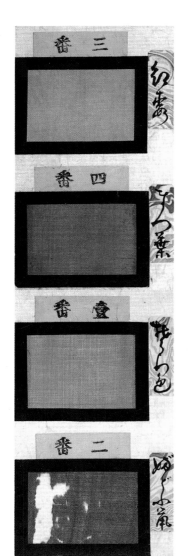

Another characteristic of the Japanese approach to art during this period was the relative lack of a hierarchical approach to artistic mediums. An artist could both make paintings and design costumes. The Western distinction between fine and applied art was not relevant. The Chinese belief in the nobility of painting, poetry and calligraphy did not prevent the Japanese from painting landscapes or dyeing calligraphic poems on clothing, all in the name of fashion and style. Artists, who are well-known for working in other mediums, but who were also involved with costume or who had training in that field, include Ogata Kōrin, Hishikawa Moronobu (prints, died 1694), Kusumi Morikage (paintings, 1620-90), Nishikawa Sukenobu (prints, 1671-1750), and Sakai Hōitsu (paintings, 1761-1828). Costume was also a favorite subject in paintings and prints.

Not surprisingly, in Japanese art similarities can be seen between styles of painting, costume design, and in the decoration of lacquer, ceramics and metalwork.

THE TEXTILE INDUSTRY

T he textile industry, as it related to the production of costly garments, included cultivators of silk, reelers of silk thread, dyers, weavers, stencil-makers, embroiderers, golf leaf and metal thread specialists, artists, tailors, and various merchants who acted as brokers and retailers in the course of the making and selling of the goods. From the sixteenth century and through the Tokugawa rule, the textile industry was subject to the same forces that shaped the society as a whole.

Kyoto, the home of the Imperial court, had been the traditional center for the luxury textile industry. However, during the civil war period, Sakai,

Right :
The dyeing of cloth for use in *kosode* is shown in this scene from a screen painting. The artisan standing in front of the tiny *kosode* patterns on the wall is using a stencil in the application of paste which will serve as a resist in the dyeing of the bolt of cloth. The squatting woman is immersing cloth in a dye bath. In the foreground, a freshly dyed cloth is stretched out prior to being hung up to dry on the latticework above the shop.

Numerous dyehouses such as the one depicted here formed a vital part of the textile industry and were responsible for many of the innovations in textile technology.

At least two virtually identical versions of this scene are represented in earlier screen paintings.

Each panel 22 ¾ × 16 ½ in. (57.7 × 42.1 cm).

Suntory Museum of Art, Tokyo.

Left :
This 18th century woodblock print depicts a courtesan wearing a *kosode* with motifs of gentians and irises, associated with the month of June.

25 × 12 in. (63.5 × 30.5 cm).
c. 1714, by Kaigetsudō Dohan (Norishige).

The University of Michigan Museum of Art, Bequest of Margaret Watson Parker, 1955/1.128.

a port near Osaka, replaced Kyoto as the textile center because of its safety relative to the turmoil of the war-torn Imperial city. Also because of its harbor, it had easy access to textile imports. Textile imports consisted of both silk thread and finished textiles, mostly coming from China. Silk thread was the single most valuable item in Japan's foreign trade during the period of European contact. When trade declined after *sakoku* was instituted, silk continued to be an important trade item, as Engelbrecht Kaempfer, a Dutchman who was in Japan from 1690-92 observed, "of all the imported goods, raw silk is the best liked".[16] Silk had been mentioned as a prestige import in the sumptuary law of 1713 quoted previously.

Finished textiles, mostly Chinese in origin, had an important influence on Japan's textile industry. Various new techniques were learned by studying imported textiles, and from Chinese textile artisans who may have settled in Japan. New techniques included improvements in the application of metallic foil on fabric (*surihaku*), the use of metallic paper strips in woven cloth (*ginran* and *kinran*), and the weaving of crepe (*chirimen*) and satin-weave figured silk (*rinzu*). These techniques were copied by the Japanese and applied in creative ways, resulting in unique textiles for use in fine garments.

Dyeing was more developed in Japan than either weaving or embroidery, and consequently there was less to be learned from abroad in that area. João Rodrigues, the Portuguese interpreter, was quite impressed by Japanese dyeing.

"And the Japanese are extremely skillful in this matter of dyeing their robes of silk and other cloth ; they intermingle gold among the flowers painted in diverse ways, and they are especially clever in their use of crimson and, even more, of violets."[17]

Towards the end of the seventeenth century, techniques and materials used in both painting and dyeing were combined, creating a method of textile decoration (*yūzen*) that was uniquely Japanese.

In the course of political unification, Kyoto was reestablished as the home of the luxury textile industry. Weaving ateliers gravitated to the Nishijin district of Kyoto. As Japan prospered, so did Nishijin. By the end of the seventeenth century, over 7,000 looms were in operation. Sumptuary laws and competition from other regional textile centers had an adverse

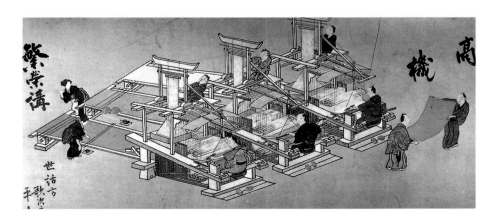

A weaving atelier in the Nishijin section of Kyoto, which became the center for the production of luxury woven fabrics.
The draw looms shown here were used in making textiles such as the figured silks used for *kosode*, and compound-weave silks for Nō costumes and *kesa*.
Collection of Nishijin-ori Kaikan, Kyoto.

effect on Nishijin's business. The sumptuary laws, enforced as part of the reforms to the Tempō era (1830-44) in an effort to stabilize the economy, were very damaging to Nishijin. The reforms outlawed the locally-based guilds, which had been exercising monopolistic control over segments of the industry, and also restricted the wearing of silk among the general population.

Regional textile centers had developed under daimyo patronage, often developing a reputation for a particular textile speciality. One such center, located in Kiryu, became an effective rival of Nishijin in the nineteenth century because it was closer to the major market, namely Edo, and was also nearer to the rural silk-producing areas. Perhaps the most serious blow to Nishijin was the forced opening of Japan to the outside world in 1853, through the efforts of Commodore Perry and the Americans. The foreign demand for Japanese silk thread made its price virtually prohibitive for Japan's own textile industry ; and the importance of traditional Japanese dress declined as the country strove to westernize its ways.

NOTES

1. Donald Shively, "Sumptuary Regulations and Status in Early Tokugawa Japan," *Harvard Journal of Asiatic Studies*, vol. 25, 1964-65, p. 128 (trans. by E.S. Crawcour).
2. J.E. de Becker, *The Nightless City ; or the History of Yoshiwara Yūkawa*, Yokohama, Z.P. Maruya & Co., 1899, p. 72.
3. Shively, op. cit., pp. 124-125 (trans. by G.W. Sargent).
4. Toshiko Itō, *Tsujigahana : The Flower of Japanese Textile Art,* trans. by Monica Bethe, New York, Kodansha International, Ltd, 1981.
5. Hayao Ishimura, Nobuhiko Maruyama, and Tomoyuki Yamanobe, *Robes of Elegance : Japanese Kimonos of the 16th-20th Centuries*, trans. by Haruko Ward, Raleigh, North Carolina Museum of Art, 1988, p. 11.
6. Saikaku Ihara, *Five Women Who Loved Love*, trans. by Wm. Theodore de Bary, Rutland, Vermont, Charles E. Tuttle Co., 1986, p. 31.
7. Miyeko Murase, *Tales of Japan : Scrolls and Prints from The New York Public Library*, New York, Oxford University Press, 1986, p. 216.
8. Donald Keene, *Nō : Classical Theater of Japan*, Tokyo, Kodansha, 1966, p. 49.
9. Shively, op. cit., p. 127.
10. Ibid.
11. Ihara, op. cit., p. 211.
12. Langdon Warner, *The Enduring Art of Japan*, New York, Grove Press, 1958, pp. 71-72.
13. Saikaku Ihara, "Two Samurai Tales", trans. by Richard Lane, *Perspective of Japan : An Atlantic Monthly Supplement*, 1954, p. 31.
14. S.J. Michael Cooper, ed., *They Came to Japan : An Anthology of European Reports on Japan, 1543-1640*, Berkeley, University of California Press, 1965, p. 206.
15. Beatrix von Ragué, "A Pair of Screens with the 'Southern Barbarians'" *The Bulletin of the Cleveland Museum of Art*, vol. 52, no. 2, Feb. 1965, p. 31 (trans. by C.R. Boxer).
16. Engelbert Kaempfer, *The History of Japan...*, 2 vols., trans. by J.G. Scheuchzer, London, Scheuchzer, 1727, p. 353.
17. S.J. Michael Cooper, ed., loc. cit.

Kosode
The High Fashion Garment

Pages 32-33 :
There is seemingly little in the way of motifs and techniques that does not appear in this *kosode*. The ground fabric is a pattern-weave silk ; gold foil was used for minutely scaled abstract, floral and animal motifs ; *shibori* dyeing produced the large areas of color and the spotted abstract and cherry tree images ; faint ink-drawn flowers are also in evidence ; and finally, tiny embroidered stitches were used to create outdoor scenes, family crests and geometric patterns.

The spotted and inked cherry blossoms outscale the adjacent embroidered cranes and pine trees. The red, white and black areas highly irregular in shape, and the overall coloration has a darkness to it that adds to the ambiguity that is characteristic of the Keichō style.

Early 17th century.

Kanebō Co., Ltd., Osaka.

THE EMERGENCE OF THE *KOSODE*

Prior to Japan's westernization beginning in the second half of the nineteenth century, *kosode* was the general term used for the garment that today is called a kimono. The literal translation of kimono is "a thing for wearing," and, in that sense, it is a generic word equivalent to 'clothing'. In popular usage, it serves as the stereotypical word for what is considered to be the traditional native dress of Japan. *Kosode* has a much more specific literal meaning, translating as "small sleeve." *Kosode* sleeves are actually quite voluminous compared to sleeves on Western clothing. However, the adjective 'small' refers to the relatively narrow openings for the hands created by sewing the outer vertical edges of the sleeves up to a point just below the shoulder line.

The *kosode* had been an upper-class undergarment over which was worn the *ōsode* (literally "large sleeve"), a robe with sleeve edges that were unsewn at the wrists. The *ōsode*-type sleeve allowed for the exposure of successive sleeve edges on the multiple robes worn by courtiers in medieval times. Color combinations were the aim of this multi-layered dressing, and the wearer's sophistication was judged by the juxtaposition of the slivers of color revealed at the sleeve edges and lapels from as many as fifteen layers of clothing.

The *ōsode* were stiff and rather cumbersome garments, especially when worn in layers. The samurai class, which had gained ascendancy over the increasingly decadent aristocracy late in the twelfth century, favored the more pliable *kosode* as an everyday informal outer robe more suited to their active lives and plebeian origins. The lower classes were already using the *kosode* as an outer garment. Impoverishment during the civil wars obliged the courtiers to adopt this simpler mode of dress. The *kosode* then became established as the informal outer robe for all classes. The wearing of two or more *kosode*, in specific combinations, became an accepted style of formal dress.

KOSODE : FORM AND FUNCTION

The *kosode*, in its role as an outer garment, had to meet certain practical and aesthetic requirements. It had to be adaptable to the seasons, and for this reason was worn unlined in the summer (*hitoemono*), lined in the spring and fall (*awase*), and lined and padded in winter (*wata-ire*). Some kind of pocket was necessary, and this need was met by the partially sewn sleeve edges, which allowed the volumnious sleeves to function also as carrying pouches. As an outer robe, the *kosode* was made extra long to cover the long undergarments and to allow for footwear, such as the often-worn high-soled wooden *geta*. The hem of the *kosode* was sometimes padded in order to give it extra weight and thereby provide the more elegant draping required of a robe worn as an outer garment. Because the neck, and especially its nape, was considered to be highly suggestive, the *kosode* collar was wide, drawing attention to that part of the body.

One practical consideration that was unaccounted for on the *kosode* was a system of fastening. For this purpose, the left side of the robe was drawn over the right and a sash (*obi*) was tied around the *kosode*.

TYPES OF *KOSODE*

Various types of *kosode* exist, dating from the mid-sixteenth through to the mid-nineteenth centuries, all having the small sleeve openings. However, some types of *kosode* served as an under-robe in combination with another *kosode*. Of the six basic types, three were worn primarily by the samurai class. Samurai families, especially those from the upper levels, followed a long tradition of preserving their treasured possessions, including fine garments, whereas the lower classes were more likely to wear out or recycle their *kosode*. Consequently, the majority of intact surviving kosode were those worn by the samurai classes.

The most distinctively shaped *kosode* is known as a *furisode* (literally "swinging sleeves"). It is characterized by sleeves that are very long in the vertical direction and are sewn to the main body of the robe with a seam beginning at the shoulder line and continuing for only a small part of the overall sleeve length. This allowed the sleeves to sway freely when worn. Other types of *kosode* can have this kind of sleeve. However, the *furisode* is further distinguished by colors and patterns that are suitable for young people and ground fabrics made of a variety of weaves, including *rinzu* (figured satin-weave silk), the most common *kosode* material. By the end of the eighteenth century, *furisode* sleeves reached their maximum length, touching the ground when worn. In the nineteenth century, *furisode* were popular as wedding attire, often worn in sets of three, with each *furisode* in a different background color.

The *uchikake* is usually made of *rinzu* and can have either long (for young people) or regular length sleeves. It was worn over another *kosode*. The designs tend to be elaborate, since the *uchikake* was worn by the samurai class on formal occasions. Being an unbelted over-robe, the hem is likely to have extra padding, adding weight to the garment to keep it from slipping off the shoulders.

A summer over-robe favored by the samurai class was the *koshimaki*. Its ground fabric has a plain-weave structure and was dyed a dark color. The *koshimaki* is densely embroidered with small-scale auspicious motifs. Its literal translation, "waist wrap," refers to the custom of wearing the robe off the shoulders and draped over the *obi* tied at the waist. The sleeve lengths of *koshimaki* can be varied.

A *hitoe* is one kind of samurai-class garment traditionally worn beneath the *koshimaki*. It is usually, of *rō*, a kind of gauze-weave silk, or *chirmen* (crepe), and unlined, making it ideal from summer wear. The sleeves may be varied in length.

The *katabira* is the only non-silk *kosode*, being made of ramie, or bast fiber. It is also an unlined summer garment. The upper level of the samurai class favored *katabira* dyed by a painstaking process developed in the eighteenth century known as *chayazome*. These robes were usually worn in combination with *koshimaki*. *Katabira* other than the *chayzome* sort were presumably worn by lower-rank samurai, townspeople and courtesans. Once again,the vertical sleeve length was not specific.

The type of *kosode* most often encountered is confusingly labelled *kosode*. Its sleeves are regular in length, rather than extra long ; it is lined, distinguishing it from the *hitoe* and *katabira* ; and it does not share the specific characteristics of the *uchikake* or the *koshimaki*. The *kosode* sleeve changed in shape, widening in the horizontal direction after the sixteenth century. Another post-sixteenth century change occurred in the narrowing of the lapels and body.

To avoid confusion, it is best to remember that *kosode* in the general sense refers to a robe with relatively small openings at the sleeve edges. A *kosode* in the specific sense is a similar garment that has sleeves of regular size, as measured in the vertical direction, and is not one of the other five types previously mentioned.

KOSODE STYLES

Styles of *kosode* decoration have been named after textile techniques, historical eras and names of people and places. In one instance, the derivation of the name of a style is unknown. Most of the styles were named well after they were in fashion, in an attempt to classify the very diverse and extensive range of extant *kosode*. Naturally, not every *kosode* fits into a specific stylistic category. There are overlaps and transitions between styles, not to mention disagreement as to the exact elements of a particular style. With this in mind, the salient characteristics of each major style found in extant *kosode* of the mid-sixteenth through mid-nineteenth centuries will be presented.

Nuihaku

Nuihaku is one of the two earliest categories of *kosode* styles. The term is derived from the words for embroidery (*nui*) and metal foil (*haku*). *Nuihaku* reflected the influence of Chinese textile technology and was, in

"Yearly, on December 8th, but more generally on February 8th, services for broken needles were held... the needle being regarded as if it were [a] living [being] whose body has been sacrificed in service. An altar consisting of two or three tiers was set up... On the top tier offerings of cake and fruit were placed. On the second step was a plate on which is a cube of tofu (bean-curd) – a jelly-like substance – into which the broken and crooked needles were thrust, the idea being to give the needles a soft rest after their hard service. A case with sewing supplies was placed at the foot of the altar." [1]

Nuihaku kosode were decorated by means of embroidery and metallic foil. It is the most traditional of the various *kosode* styles that flourished between the mid-16th through the mid-19th centuries.

Nuihaku design formats are symmetrical, featuring alternating blocks of colors and/or patterns, and were inspired by earlier costumes that were pieced together from the salvaged parts of worn-out garments.

This *kosode*'s design is divided into quarters with color schemes that are similar along the diagonal axis. Each quarter represents a season. Beginning with the upper right quarter and reading counter-clockwise, fall, winter, spring and summer are symbolized by maple leaves, bamboo leaves, plum blossoms and wisteria, respectively.

The embroidery stitches and the application of gold leaf were based on Chinese textile techniques. The silk ground fabric is a kind of plain weave called *nerinuki*. It is completely covered by the embroidery and gilding, some of which has now worn off.

After falling out of favor as a *kosode* style in the beginning of the 17th century, the *nuihaku* had continued life as a costume type in the Nō theater.

Latter half of the 16th century.

part, a response to the disruption of the *sengoku* period. The embroidery of *nuihaku* was modelled after a popular Chinese Ming Dynasty (1368-1644) stitch called *watashi* by the Japanese. *Watashi* employed unspun and degummed silk threads (sericin, the sticky substance that adheres to the silk filaments unwound from coccons, is removed, producing a soft floss thread) in long stitches which can span the breadth of individual motifs. Short transverse stitches were used sparingly to secure the long stitches, while also providing details to the motifs. Reds, yellows and greens are the dominant colors of the embroidered motifs, which are tightly spaced and surrounded by metallic foil, creating a rich and sumptuous appearance.

The application of gold and silver foil onto fabric was also copied from the Chinese. The metallic foil was secured by paste and applied either freehand or with the aid of stencils in a technique called *surihaku*. An imported Chinese fabric known as *inkin* in Japanese was probably the model for *surihaku*. An adaptation made in Japan resulted in the substitution of *nerinuku* (a balanced plain-woven fabric with raw silk warps and degummed silk wefts) for the silk gauze usually employed in *inkin*. The applied metallic foil used in combination with embroidery in *nuihaku* was probably a substitution for the rounded metallic threads often used together with silk thread embroidery in Chinese textiles.

Nuihaku was also a practical response to the economic and industrial dislocations of the civil war period. Imported Chinese silks became scarce and expensive in Japan and the native textile industry was too disrupted to attempt the large-scale production of fine-woven versions of Chinese textiles. The textile that *nuihaku* most closely resembles is known as *karaori* (literally "Chinese weave") in Japanese. *Karaori* is a woven textile known for its long floating wefts which are reminiscent of embroidery and for its gilded or silvered strips of paper which are also used as wefts, sometimes filling spaces between motifs in the same way that metallic foil does in *nuihaku*. *Nuihaku* was not only a cheaper and simpler version of *karaori*, since it did not require the slow and complicated drawloom weaving process, but it also had the advantage of greater design flexibility afforded by freehand embroidery and applied foil, as compared to the mechanical restrictions of loom weaving.

The design formats of *nuihaku kosode* have their origins in the cost-cutting measures necessitated by economic hardship ; and they share a certain similarity with the repeat patterns that are characteristic of woven textiles. *Dan gawari* (alternating blocks of similar patterns), *katami gawari* (the right half patterned differently from the left half), and *sode gawari* (sleeves in a pattern different from the body) formats originally resulted from the piecing together of the best preserved sections of two different garments. *Kata suso*, an empty-centered format with the same pattern concentrated at the shoulders and hem, allowed for the reduction of labor and materials in the making of a *kosode*. Such formats also recalled the repeat patterns of more costly woven fabrics. When prosperity came in the second half of the sixteenth century, these formats were no longer necessary. However, the striking juxtaposition of differing patterns and colors became fashionable, and *nuihaku kosode* were designed in this manner rather than patched together as before.

Nuihaku fell out of favor as a *kosode* style in the seventeenth century, but it had a long second life after it was adopted as one of the principal types of Nō costumes. Having been a popular samurai class garment, it was therefore appropriate for use in a theater form patronized by that class.

Tsujigahana

Tsujigahana, the other dominant *kosode* style of the latter half of the sixteenth century, is considered to have had its antecedents in the pattern-dyed garments associated with the lower classes, as opposed to the Chinese-influenced weaving derived *nuihaku* technique, with its upper-class origins. *Tsujigahana* therefore represents the first native trend to emerge in *kosode* during the period under consideration, and perhaps that accounts for its popularity to this day.

"Spring gusts –

One hand steadies

a bucket of fresh fish

The other a sleeve

of tsujigahana".[2]

Sanjūniban Shokunin Utawase (Song Competition of Thirty-two Trades), late 14th/early 15th century.

A front view of a *tsujigahana kosode* dated by inscription to 1566. Ink painting and gilding, two other techniques that were sometimes elements of the *tsujigahana* style, are used in this example.

The ink painting appears in the bands between the dyed areas, which were once a bright red, but are now faded to a light brown color. The sophisticated painting of flowers and birds exhibits the shading that is characteristic of *hakubyō* style brushwork.

Gold foil, only traces of which have survived, was applied in the dyed areas to highlight the floral motifs that were originally traced in ink.

The *kata-suso* format is followed here, although on the back of the garment decoration appears only at the shoulders. The shape of *kosode* was to change in the following century as sleeves became wider and the body and lapels narrower.

Latter half of the 16th century.
Tokyo National Museum.

Tsujigahana kosode fragments have been mounted on a folding screen to appear as if they are garments draped over a rack. The inspiration for this collage are the *tagasode* screen paintings of *kosode*.
Shibori techniques that involved stitching and wrapping to protect against dye penetration have been used to create the motifs on these fragments. The piece on the right also exhibits the shading of *hakubyō* ink painting.
Late 16th/early 17th century
Normura Collection. Photo courtesy of Tokyo National Museum.

Tsujigahana, as it is understood today, was first used in the latter half of the nineteenth century as a costume and textile term. No consensus exists as to the original meaning of the word, or its derivation. There is, however, general agreement as to which *kosode* reflect this style.

Tsujigahana, like *nuihaku*, also employs plain-weave *nerinuki* as a base fabric, and can include embroidery and metallic foil. However, its most noted technical feature is a kind of resist dyeing known as *shibori*. There are several varieties of *shibori*, but most involve stitching off the outlines of motifs or any areas that are not meant to receive a particular dye. To prevent dye penetration, the stitched-off part is wrapped with relatively dye-resistant fiber or otherwise covered and protected during the immersion dyeing process. *Shibori* can produce everything from minute spots to broad areas of different coloration. *Shibori* is always present in *tsujigahana*, and in some examples it is the sole means of decoration.

The other most characteristic technique associated with *tsujigahana*, although not found in every example, is brush painting using inks which are pigments rather than dyes. The painting is either *hakubyō*-style, known for its delicate shaded outlines, or *suiboku-ga*, with its more precise thin and thick lines. Both kinds of ink painting were employed in album, scroll and screen paintings of the time.[3] Names of specific artists who participated in the *tsujigahana* process are no longer known, making direct associations with attributed works in the other mediums impossible. However, the high quality of painting in *tsujigahana* and its close resemblance to other extant ink paintings indicate that artistic interchanges must have taken place.

Page 41 :
Characteristics of the *tsujigahana* and *nuihaku* styles are combined in this garment, which is classified as a Nō theater garment today. Prior to the time when Nō costumes were made specifically for use on the stage, it had been customary to present an actor with a luxurious garment in appreciation of a fine performance.
The *nuihaku* sections, which are on the darker red background, have the long floating embroidery stitches and foil decoration (now barely visible) that are typical of *nuihaku kosode*. The other parts of the robe, featuring motifs consisting of flowers, grids, pools of water and rectangular-shaped decorated paper, are patterned by means of *shibori* and foil work in the *tsujigahana* style. The alternating format is most often seen in *nuihaku kosode*. Here, the sleeves differ, as do diagonally opposed sections of the body, creating a rhythmic overall design effect.
Latter half of the 16th century.
Tokyo National Museum.

Tsujigahana also shares an affinity with two other artistic mediums of the period, lacquer and ceramics. Motifs found in lacquerware associated with the Rimpa school and pottery known as Oribe, after the tea master, resemble some motifs found in *tsujigahana*.[4]

Design formats of *tsujigahana kosode* can be similar to those of *nuihaku kosode*. The earliest dated *kosode* of the period, with an inscription from 1566, is in *tsujigahana* style, having a dyed shoulder-hem design format. Individual motifs can be closely spaced, as in *nuihaku*, but more often they are evenly scattered. A wider range of color is found in *tsujigahana* as compared to *nuihaku*. Also, with a greater variety of techniques to draw upon, *tsujigahana* garments are more varied in appearance than *nuihaku kosode*.

Surviving *tsujigahana kosode* are likely to have been samurai-class garments. In fact, several of the few intact examples once belonged to Toyotomi Hideyoshi and Tokugawa Ieyasu. These two leaders also owned *tsujigahana* garments other than *kosode*, as did other important samurai. It is possible that the lower classes also may have worn *tsujigahana* ; this is based on evidence that has been found in genre paintings of the time.[5] Paintings from earlier periods show pattern-dyed garments being worn by the lower classes,[6] who would naturally have been unable to afford costlier weave-patterned clothing. It is likely that the pattern dyeing which existed in Japan, as evidenced from paintings, strongly influenced the dyeing of *tsujigahana* garments. Extant fragments of *tsujigahana* which exhibit less precise, more blurred *shibori*-dyed motifs, are thought to represent a poorer quality *tsujigahana* worn by the lower classes.[7] However, the more blurred effect could have been a deliberate upper-class attempt to add a touch of naiveté to an otherwise fashionable garment.[8] As such, it would have been aesthetically comparable to the desire for a mood of rustic simplicity during a performance of the highly refined tea ceremony.

Tsujigahana degenerated as a *kosode* style in the seventeenth century, when it was combined with the *nuihaku* style and when it was worked on a ground fabric of woven figured silk, such as *rinzu*. As mentioned earlier, *tsujigahana* could include *nuihaku* techniques and ink painting, along with *shibori*, but usually did so to a limited extent. When the metallic foil and embroidered areas became more extensive, as in *nuihaku kosode*, the subtle balance between different techniques in *tsujigahana* was adversely affected. The style was also diluted when figured silks became the favored *kosode* material. *Rinzu*, another Chinese import later copied in Japan, was woven in a satin weave and degummed after weaving, making it easier to dye, softer to touch, and looser in drape than the plain-woven *nerinuki* with its raw silk wefts. The patterning of figured silk proved to be a distraction in *tsujigahana*, especially when ink painting was involved. Even so, the advantages of figured silk as a *kosode* material were considered to more than compensate for the negative impact it had on the appearance of *tsujigahana*. The eagerness with which the new fabric was employed was a sign that *tsujigahana* was falling out of favor as a *kosode* style.

Keichō

The later experiments with *nuihaku* and *tsujigahana* had a successful resolution in the so-called Keichō style. This style takes its name from the Keichō *nengō* (a *nengō* is a time period used in Japanese chronology), which lasted from 1596 to 1615. The Keichō designation is misleading because the style is more prevalent on *kosode* that are thought to date to the second quarter of the seventeenth century. However, only a handful of complete Keichō *kosode* have survived, so it is mainly through fragments that the style is known.

Keichō style *kosode* continued to exhibit most of the same technical characteristics of the two styles that preceded it, but with significant variations. *Rinzu* was firmly established as the *kosode* fabric of preference by this time and consequently ink painting became a rare feature of this style, in contrast to the earlier *tsujigahana*. Metallic foil was used more freely and creatively than in the *nuihaku*, depicting various individual motifs instead of primarily filling in areas between embroidered motifs. Unfortunately, much of the foil originally used on Keichō *kosode* has worn off over time and is nowadays barely visible. Rounded gold or silver threads, made by wrapping gilded or silvered strips of paper around a silk thread, were an additional metallic element incorporated in Keichō *kosode*. These threads had to be couched on the surface of the fabric since they were too bulky to pass through it safely. *Shibori* dyeing was also used more freely than before, delineating large, irregular shapes, as well as smaller motifs. Minute motifs were rendered in embroidery.

The Keichō style is most strikingly different from preceding and following styles in its asymmetrical design, coloration and in the ambiguity of its pattern. Design layouts departed from the symmetry of earlier styles and moved towards more varied formats, usually having a diagonal thrust. *Shibori* was used to create the broad areas of different color that are a major component of this style. The dyed colors are predominantly red and black, giving Keichō style *kosode* an overall dark appearance. Although small-scale embroidered motifs were originally brighter, as with many dyed colors, they have faded with age. This fading, along with the loss of metallic foil, has contributed to the dark look of Keichō *kosode*.

As in the earlier styles, motifs taken from nature predominate, but their proportions are sometimes the reverse of what would normally be expected. Flowers are larger than birds and clouds, fans dwarf trees, contributing to the overall sense of abstraction which, along with the irregularity of the dyed areas, create an ambiguity in the relationship between figures and background. The complexity inherent in this style limited it to the samurai class or very cultivated *chōnin* who were able to interpret the allusions to Chinese and Japanese medieval literature that are sometimes present on these *kosode*.

Another very noticeable change that appears in the Keichō style is in the shape of the *kosode*, which has now become horizontally wider in the sleeves and narrower in the body and lapels. This shape was continued in subsequent styles, including the Kanbun style that succeeded it.

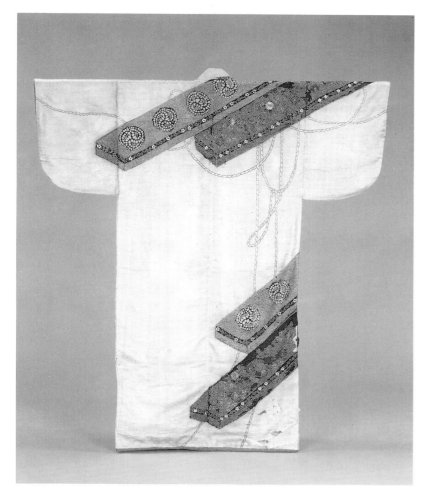

"Kanbun 'bijin' (beauties of the Kanbun era) is a generic term referring to paintings of beautiful women in solitary splendor... layers of brilliantly designed robes accentuate their delicate beauty."[10]

Kanbun

Kanbun *kosode* are also named after a *nengō*, a period covering the years from 1661 to 1673. Extant *kosode* which most typify this style are considered to have been produced within this period. They feature a bold, sweeping design format that stretches asymmetrically from the left sleeve to the hem. The spaces between motifs are left undecorated, as are the relatively large sections of the *kosode* that do not contain the dramatic, sweeping design. The motifs are executed in *shibori* and embroidery, with little or no metallic foil or ink painting used. Rounded metallic threads and *shibori*-dyed spots (named *kanoko* after the spots on deer) are more prevalent than in Keichō *kosode*. The outlines of larger *shibori*-dyed motifs are often embroidered over, covering the blurred edges created by *shibori*, and adding to the sharpness and definition of the already bold and conspicuous design.

Drawings and printed books of the period are a source of further information about Kanbun *kosode*, providing a more complete view of the style than can be gleaned from the few existing intact *kosode*. Several hundred drawings from the Kariganeya clothing atelier in Kyoto record designs, materials, colors and techniques used in *kosode* made for Tō

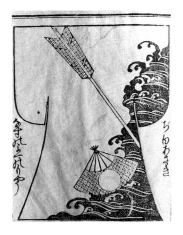

Two pages from a *hiinagata bon* (*kosode* design book) that is dated to the seventh year of the Kanbun era (equivalent to 1667). Costume design books were first published in quantity during that time. They provide a more complete view of the full range of Kanbun style *kosode*, since few *kosode* of the period are extant.
7 × 4 ⅞ in. (17.7 × 12.5 cm).
Carl Nomura Collection.

Page 44, right :
The written character as a *kosode* motif is cleverly presented in this painting. The theme of the robe is the board game called *shōgi*, which is played on a grid using tiles marked with characters. In choosing this theme, the painter might be making a pun concerning the woman depicted, since a word for courtesan is also pronounced " *shōgi.* "
31 ¼ × 15 ⅝ in.
Nonoguchi Ryuchō (1595-1669).
The Seattle Art Museum, Eugene Fuller Memorial Collection, 60.80

fukumon-in and her retainers. She was the daughter of shogun Tokugawa Hidetada, and a consort of Emperor Gomizuno-o. The drawings are dated throughout the Kanbun years and conform with the stylistic features of extant *kosode*.[11] They also cast doubt on the theory that the sparser Kanbun design format had been instituted as a labor and cost-saving measure in response to the devastating fires of 1657 in Edo and 1661 in Kyoto. The Kariganeya atelier was located in Kyoto, and presumably the *kosode* represented in their drawings were made there. Since the first group of drawings are dated 1661, but prior to the date the Kyoto fire, its destructive effects could not have influenced the designs that they depicted. Also, the fact that designs in the same style prevailed in drawings made later in the Kanbun period, when the damaged sections of Kyoto would have been rebuilt, is further evidence of the popularity and persistence of this style for its own sake.

It is interesting to note that the owner of Kariganeya was the father of the well-known artists Kōrin and Kenzan, celebrated for painting and pottery respectively. The owner probably oversaw and helped design the *kosode* produced by his atelier, and undoubtedly his sons worked there, since it has always been customary in Japan for sons to continue their fathers' work. This might explain the fact that the imaginative style of Kanbun *kosode* is also evident in Kōrin's painting and Kenzan's pottery.

Printed order books of *kosode* designs (*hiinagata bon*) are extant from the Kanbun period and, judging from the number of books that have survived, these were first produced in quantity. The design books were one variety of woodblock prints known as ukiyoe, an art form that was encouraged by the *chōnin* and denizens of the licensed districts. They were circulated and used by townspeople, courtesans and their clothiers for design inspiration.

The designs in *hiinagata bon* correlate with the Kariganeya drawings and extant *kosode* in terms of style, and provide evidence that this mode was popular with lower classes as well as with samurai society.

As mentioned earlier, the preservation of family valuables was a samurai custom, and therefore Kanbun *kosode* that have survived intact, most likely belonged to members of this class. However, all classes followed the custom of donating clothing to Buddhist temples, where they were made into *kesa* and temple furnishings. Some Kanbun *kosode* have been reassembled from temple cloths, and it is possible that several of these garments originally belonged to members of the lower classes.

Desing motifs in Kanbun *kosode* continued the literary allusions first seen in Keichō *kosode*. Chinese characters (*kanji*), which have always been the basis of the Japanese system of writing, often serve as clues to a particular poem or legend being referred to. Visually, Chinese script was well suited to the Kanbun design format, since the characters were usually rendered in a flowing calligraphic hand when used in literary works. Many of the *kosode* designs in *hiinagata bon* include *kanji*, indicating that the lower classes were also fond of literary allusions. Prosperity, urbanization and greater literacy, fostered by the growing publishing industry, had created a larger and more sophisticated audience for creative *kosode*.

Page 45 :
A single motif is arrayed as if it were a sequential image frozen in various positions as it moved through space. A simple type of net used for scooping is an unusual choice as the sole motif for a *kosode*. It may have been chosen for its resemblance to a fan, which has always been a popular image in Japanese art. Also, the scoop net was a rustic object that probably evoked the simpler past of a formerly agrarian Japan, now on its way toward urbanization.
The *shibori* dyeing, couched metallic threads, polychrome embroidery and *rinzu* are the materials and techniques seen here that are typical of the Kanbun style.
Deterioration of the fabric in the areas that have been dyed in black was caused by the use of a corrosive element such as iron in the dyeing process.
Latter half of the 17th century.
Tokyo National Museum.

Genroku

The Genroku style takes its name from the *nengō* spanning the years 1688 to 1704 ; however, the style persisted on into the middle of the eighteenth century. The sweep of the Kanbun design format was continued, but was widened to a point where undecorated areas were confined primarily to the center portion of the left rear and front panels of the *kosode*. More of the design appeared on the front of the robe, as well as the shoulders and hem. The widening of the *obi* (sash), which began in this period and gradually increased thereafter, was an influence on the new, fuller format. The increased width of the *obi* now had to be considered when designing motifs for the areas above and below those covered by the sash. This led to the creation of design formats in which the motifs at the shoulders differed from those on the lower half of the robe. Another design format, which worked well with the wider *obi*, featured the repetition of similar motifs ranging from the shoulders to the hem, thereby eliminating uncertainity as to what lay covered by the sash.

Technical changes from the preceding Kanbun style were few in number. Tighter embroidery stitches, such as satin stitch, were used more frequently on Genroku *kosode*, as were methods of imitating the appearance of spotted *shibori*. Instead of wrapping minute areas of fabric in order to create a resist for the dyeing of the *kanoko* motif, a paper stencil

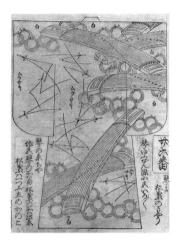

A page from *Nishikawa hiinagata* (1718) showing a typical example of the Genroku style. The notations on the design provide color suggestions for the background. The string instrument represented is called a *koto*.
8 ⅝ × 5 ⅝ in. (22 × 14.5 cm).
Spencer Collection, The New York Public Library. Astor, Lenox and Tilden Foundations.

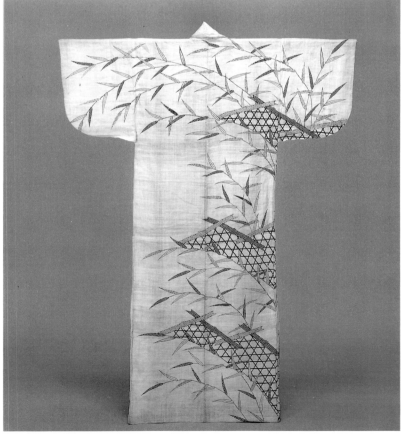

Right :
A suggestive print by Utamaro (1753-1806) showing a courtesan tying a wide *obi* with the star pattern over a *kosode* with an overall design of birds and clouds.
Courtesan Hana Ōgi of Ogiya, woodblock print.
Charles Stewart Smith Collection. Miriam and Ira D. Wallach Division of Art, Prints and Photographs. The New York Public Library. Astor, Lenox and Tilden Foundations.

Page 46 :
Two views illustrate how a design wraps around the front and back of a *kosode*. Diagonal designs such as this one required careful planning and execution in order for the motifs to match precisely across the many seams traversed by the pattern. This is all the more remarkable considering that all *kosode* originated from a single length of fabric.
The design on this *katabira* type of *kosode* depicts water reeds and basketry used to shore up river embankments. Such images would be appropriately cooling for a summer garment.
First half of the 18th century.
Tokyo National Museum.

was cut out with a series of holes. Paste was applied through the stencil, which resisted the dye during immersion. Once the paste was washed off, an ink dot was usually applied to the center of each spot in further imitation of spotted *shibori*. An alternate method involved the rubbing of a crayon made of pigment and wax directly over the stencil.

Design books, women's encyclopedias and fashion plates in the Genroku style were widely circulated, as the publishing industry was flourishing by that time and more and more people were interested in and able to afford fashionable clothing. Everyday objects such as hats, fences, curtains, musical instruments, and boats became popular motifs, adding a more whimsical aspect to *kosode* patterning. Unfortunately, unique and creative designs were not in unlimited supply, and the increasing demand for the best in *kosode* design could not be met. The result was the inevitable standardization and repetition of motifs, leading to the demise of the Genroku style.

"There was a painter who was called Yūzen. He painted first-class paintings on fans, which delighted men and women of all classes. Through this he came to understand peoples' taste. He created designs for the women's kosode and offered them to a certain dry goods dealer. Because he heard that these interested the people, a certain book dealer published these widely."[13]

Preface of *Onna-yō kunnō yui* (Moral Teachings for Women), 1687

Yūzen

Another *kosode* style that was popular during the Genroku years and continued to be in favor throughout the following two centuries is called *yūzen*. *Yūzen* was the end result of the search for a successful fusion of painting and dyeing that took place during the second half of the seventeenth century. The term *yūzen* derives from the name of a Kyoto painter, Miyazaki Yūzensai (d. 1711), who was known for his paintings on fans. His work also influenced *kosode* design at a time when dyers were competing to develop techniques that could expand the pictorial possibilities of their medium. The most successful method that evolved was named after the artist, and was also used in decorating objects made of paper and wood.

The traditional *yūzen* technique combined the use of pigments, brushes and a painter's skill with the dyes, mordants and pastes of a dye specialist. There are variants in the sequence of steps involved in the process; however, it can be summarized in the following way: the outlines of motifs are drawn in thin lines of rice paste. Within the outlines, the motifs are brush painted using pigments and/or dyes and mordants. For the background color, the completed motifs are covered with rice paste to protect those areas from the pigments and/or dyes and mordants, which are then applied using a thicker brush. A fixitive liquid made from soybeans is also employed in *yūzen*, in order to stabilize the pigments. The final step involves steaming the fabric, which removes the paste and aids in the binding of the colorants to the cloth. When a background color was desired that required immersion dyeing, such as blue from indigo or reddish-orange from safflower, the areas which were to be painted with motifs were first covered with paste, and then followed the immersion dyeing for the background color, after which motifs were painted in the above-mentioned manner. The creation of subtle gradations within a color area was a later refinement that added to the painterly qualitites of *yūzen*. Other textile techniques were sometimes used sparingly in combination with *yūzen*,

Below :
Chirimen, a type of crepe fabric, rather than *rinzu*, is the material used for this *kosode*. *Chirimen* was often the preferred fabric for *kosode* decorated by means of the *yūzen* technique. The sharply defined checkered pattern was achieved by means of paste resists, which were an important ingredient in the *yūzen* technique.

The paulownia leaves and blossoms are embroidered and *shibori* dyed; the faint leaves at the left center of the robe are outlined in ink keeping that portion of the *kosode* relatively undecorated, in accordance with the Genroku design format.
Late 17th/early 18th century.
Tokyo National Museum.

including *shibori*, and embroidery in silk and metallic threads. *Chirimen*, a variety of silk crepe, was the preferred fabric for *yūzen*.

The *yūzen* process produced *kosode* with finely detailed motifs in a wide range of colors that were unobtainable from previous conventional textile techniques. Although *tsujigahana kosode* were painted with pigments, black ink was the only color used. *Yūzen* is perhaps just as much a technique as a style. Because of its lengthy popularity, it was used in combination with several chronologically different *kosode* design formats. The widening *obi* had the same effect on the design layout in *yūzen kosode* as on the Genroku style *kosode*. The *yūzen* technique continued to be employed in later *kosode*, when different design formats were prevalent. However, *yūzen* merits its own stylistic category because of the greater freedom of expression allowed by this method, and because of the distinctiveness of its appearance.

With the introduction of synthetic dyes during the middle of the nineteenth century, immersion dyeing was no longer required to produce certain background colors in *yūzen kosode*. The rush to modernize led to the abandonment of traditional dyes and dyeing methods in the *yūzen* process. The disregard for the special qualities imparted to fabric through immersion dyeing was ultimately detrimental to *yūzen kosode*.

The *kosode* worn by the two women seated on the platform under the cherry tree and their two attendants reveal shading that is characteristic of some *yūzen kosode*. The painterly qualities of *yūzen kosode* made them a convenient subject for artists.
21 ⅝ × 28 ⅝ in.
(54.9 × 72.7 cm).
Painting by Matsumo Chikanobu (active 1716-35).
The Seattle Art Museum, gift of Mrs. Alfred F. Woolsey and Miss Maud Oakes in memory of their parents, Mr. and Mrs. Walter Oakes, 55.160.

Chayazome

Another painterly style, but rooted primarily in dyeing techniques, is *chayazome*. *Chaya* is said to derive from the family name of a dyer or a merchant who is thought to have lived in Kyoto during the seventeenth century ; *zome* is a suffix meaning dyeing. *Chayazome* was used exclusively on *katabira* (an unlined summer *kosode*) made for samurai-class women.

The technique, which has yet to be duplicated in modern times, required the paste-resisting of both sides of the ramie cloth, which as a bast fiber, is difficult to dye. Intricate landscape and rural scenes are the subject matter of extant *chayazome kosode*. Indigo served as the principal dye, and for certain details it was used as a pigment in crayon form mixed with wax. Multiple dippings in indigo, combined with reapplications of resist paste, produced different shades of blue. Embroidery in polychrome silk threads and metallic threads was often added for further detailing.

Extant *chayazome kosode* date to the eighteenth and nineteenth centuries, but reflect earlier tastes for rustic scenes favored by the samurai class, in contrast to the more genre-like subject matter that is occasionally seen in *yūzen kosode* and was more in keeping with *chōnin* taste.

"Shinto respect and reverence for the life in nature lives in the indigo dyer's dark workroom... For some dyers, indigo vats are sacred places where a protective deity dwells... The guardian deity of dyers is Aizen Myōō, whose name means "dyed in love"... As part of the New Year's ritual, a miniature kimono, cut from handmade paper and partially dipped in indigo dye, was traditionally offered to the deity's shrine in the dyer's shop. The dyed kimono symbolizes a request for good fortune during the coming year." [14]

Right :
Ogata Kōrin, the best-known Japanese artist of his time and a founder of the Rimpa school of painting , is thought to have painted this *kosode*. His father was a leading clothing merchant in Kyoto who supplied the shogunal houseold, among others, with stylish *kosode*.
Colored pigments were applied by brush directly onto the silk fabric. The subject is *akikusa* (" autumnal grasses "), a group of flowers and plants associated with autumn. *Akikusa* is a theme that was more prevalent in Nō costume design than *kosode* design.
This garment was purported to have been made for the wife of a wealthy merchant. If so, the patron had upper-class aspirations, since the choice of subject reflects samurai taste.
Late 17th/early 18th century.
Tokyo National Museum.

(Detail)
Thatch-roofed huts, a stream and vegetation of the four seasons are featured on this *katabira*. Such bucolic landscapes were favored by the samurai class, whose wealth and influence was declining at the expense of the urbanite merchant and artisan classes.
Chayazome is the name for the complicated process used for the decoration of this robe. This technique involved intricate applications of resist paste and the use of indigo in both dye and pigment states.
The overall effect of *chayazome* is quite subdued in comparison to the exuberance of *yūzen*.
18th century.
Tokyo National Museum.

Painted *Kosode*

A minor category of *kosode*, represented by only a handful of extant examples, are *kosode* painted by artists known for their screen, scroll and album paintings. The artists would have been familiar with silk, since it was sometimes used as a painting surface, although not as often as paper. Painters were also aware of textiles for another reason. It was standard practice to surround screen and scroll paintings with fabric borders that

"Kōrin was later again to fall foul of the authorities when the linings of the kimono worn by his womenfolk were found to have been painted by him, every stroke of whose brush cost a piece of gold to buy." [15]

were carefully chosen to complement each painting. Black and colored pigments and gold leaf, sometimes in powdered form, have been painted on *kosode* made of plain, satin or figured-weave silks. Unlike *yūzen*, no dyeing-resist pastes or dyes were used in this process.

Some of the painters who have worked on *kosode* are Ogata Kōrin (1658-1716), Gion Nankai (1676-1751), Matsumura Goshun (1752-1811) and Sakai Hoitsu (1761-1828). Their *kosode* are a testament to the versatility of the Japanese artists who applied their talent to a variety of mediums, without distinguishing between those appropriate for art or craft.

Goshodoki

The *goshodoki* style expanded on the subject matter found in *chayazome kosode*, and was also favored by samurai-class women. *Goshodoki* refers to a guessing game played at court, the object of which was to decode obscure medieval literary allusions. *Kosode* of this sort featured silk and metallic thread embroidery. When resist paste dyeing was used, the motifs were usually reserved in white, with embroidered details added after the dyeing was completed.

Samurai women were able to demonstrate their cultivation and sophistication by the subtlety of the literary allusions on their clothing. These references to the past undoubtedly reflected nostalgia for a time when the samurai class was full of vitality and had not become the anachronism that it was during the peaceful years of the Tokugawa rule.

Edozuma

The final distinct *kosode* style is known as *edozuma*, and was most popular from the mid-eighteenth to the mid-nineteenth centuries. It was named after the city of Edo, with the suffix *zuma* added, meaning 'skirt'. Characteristics of the style include bilateral symmetry across the center seam, smaller-scale motifs, and an emphasis on the design of the front of the robe.

The design formats were influenced by the ever-widening *obi*, which came to be almost as costly and important as the *kosode* itself. Motifs were either repeated in overall patterns or, as in later examples, limited to the edges of the hem, lapels and sleeves. The new design formats were carried out in all of the known techniques.

The effect of *edozuma* patterning can be quite sublime, especially when motifs are arranged at the outer edges of the *kosode*. The style may have been a reaction against the force and exuberance of previous styles. Sumptuary laws are thought to have had an influence in the toning down of *kosode* in the nineteenth century ; however it is more likely that the impact of a declining economy was responsible for the conservatism in dress. The expense and competition involved in following fashions must have become tiring. A simpler, conservative look was more suited to the realities of the

"Before leaving, he took off the three small-sleeved gowns [kosode] he was wearing and presented them to me. His Majesty murmured goodbye, and I gazed fondly after him as he retired to an inner room...

To wear your gowns –

Love tokens from the distant past,

Now tears stain dark sleeves."[16]

From *The Confessions of Lady Nijō*, written ca. 1307

"A courtesan named Shigasaki introduced the custom of wearing a broad obi *(sash) she herself having worn one 33" [84 cm.] in width... the woman who first set the fashion was known as "Obi Shigasaki" or "Obi-gokumon."*

("Sash-exposing-a-criminal's head." [It] was a joking reference to the ancient custom of exposing the severed head of an executed criminal to the public gaze : the sash was supposed to be so broad that only the head was visible above it)."[17]

time. Furthermore, the textile and costume industry had run out of the fresh ideas and new techniques that were needed to continue their past successes. Only occasionally are impressive designs seen in later *kosode*. However these tended to be of the *uchikake* type, worn without an *obi* and therefore not subject to its constraints.

Men had been dressing more conservatively since the Genroku era, wearing simple striped and geometric-patterned clothing, although sometimes with elaborate linings and under-robes. They were the first to abandon the *kosode* for Western dress in 1867 when Japan had fully embarked on the path to westernization with the overthrow of the shogunate.

Below :
Geisha, who first appeared in the mid-18th century, were in the forefront of the trend towards more subtle *kosode* designs. Subtler dress was a part of their efforts to advance themselves in the brothel hierarchy at the expense of their more elaborately clothed competitors.
15 ¼ × 10 ⅛ in.
(38.8 × 25.6 cm).
" The Geisha Itsutomi "
Woodblock print by Chōbunsai Eishi (1756-1829).
Yale University Art Gallery.
Frances Gaylord Smith Collection.

NOTES

1. Frederic de Garis, *We Japanese*, vol. 1, Hakone, Fujiya Hotel, Ltd., 1950, p. 160.
2. Toshiko Itō, *Tsujigahana : The Flower of Japanese Textile Art*, trans. by Monica Bethe, New York, Kodansha International, Ltd., 1981, p. 19.
3. Ibid, p. 90.
4. Ibid, p. 48.
5. Ibid, p. 111.
6. Seiroku Noma, *Japanese Costume and Textile Arts*, trans. by Armins Nikovskis, New York, Weatherhill/Heibonsha, 1977, p. 145.
7. Itō, loc. cit.
8. Hayao Ishimura, Nobuhiko Maruyama, and Tomoyuki Yamanobe, *Robes of Elegance : Japanese Kimonos of the 16th-20th Centuries*, trans. by Haruko Ward, Raleigh, North Carolina Museum of Art, 1988, p. 9.
9. Kenichi Kawakatsu, *Kimono*, Tokyo, Japan Travel Bureau, 1954, p. 77.
10. Miyeko Murase, *Japanese Art : Selections from the Mary and Jackson Burke Collection*, New York, The Metropolitan Museum of Art, p. 288.
11. Monica Bethe, Margot Paul, and Amanda Mayer Stinchecum, *Kosode : 16th-19th Century Textiles from the Nomura Collection*, New York, Japan Society/Kodansha International, 1984, p. 53.
12. Langdon Warner, *The Enduring Art of Japan*, New York, Grove Press, Inc., 1958, p. 71.
13. Ishimura, op. cit., p. 24.
14. Reiko Mochinaga Brandon, *Country Textiles of Japan : The Art of Tsutsugaki*, New York, John Weatherhill, Inc., 1986, pp. 51-2.
15. Warner, op. cit., p. 72.
16. Lady Nijō, *The Confessions of Lady Nijō*, trans. by Karen Brazell, Stanford, Stanford University Press, 1985, p. 208.
17. J.E. de Becker, *The Nightless City ; or the History of Yoshiwara Yūkawa*, Yokohama, Z.P. Maruya & Co., 1899, p. 141-42.

(Detail) pages 52-53 :

The *hitoe* was another kind of samurai-class *kosode*. It was usually constructed of gauze-weave silk, and worn unlined. These two features made it practical for summer use. However, custom dictated that a dense robe, such as the *koshimaki*, be worn over the *hitoe*, which would have had the unfortunate effect of counteracting the cooling properties of the *hitoe*.

This example illustrates the kind of subject matter that is identified with the *goshodoki* style. The motifs are meant to be subtle allusions to medieval literature. Here wild geese are shown in flight perched along a sandy shore. This is undoubtedly a reference to Katata, a famous scenic spot along Lake Biwa near Kyoto, that was known for its geese. Several medieval poems, as well as later literary works, celebrated this site.

Late 18th century.

Tokyo National Museum, gift of Mrs. Takagi Kyō.

(Detail)
A variety of techniques and materials were employed in the making of this *furisode*. Gold foil has been used for some of the fans, while others have been created by *shibori* dyeing. The floral, bird, tortoise, wheel and landscape images within the fans were produced by a combination of ink painting, embroidery and *yūzen* techniques. Spots representing a stream are the result of *shibori* dyeing.
Two similar *furisode*, which would have had a white and a black background, may have been worn together with this example as bridal gowns in a wedding ceremony, as was the custom during the 19th century.
First half of the 19th century.
Bunka Gakuen Costume Museum, Tokyo.

Plates

A *kosode* that can be seen as a prototype for future styles presents a dramatic sweeping design that extends from the left shoulder to the lower right hem. The bamboo leaves have detailing in ink, and *nerinuki* is the ground fabric in the tradition of *tsujigahana*.

This robe is considered to have once belonged to Tokugawa Ieyasu. His family crest, consisting of three wild ginger leaves, appears in the three small circles across the top of the garment.

The geometric pattern that is dyed in purple has been interrupted as the result of a later retailoring of the sleeves. It was a popular motif at this time and was given a fanciful name that translates as "pine bark lozenge."

Late 16th century.

Tokyo National Museum.

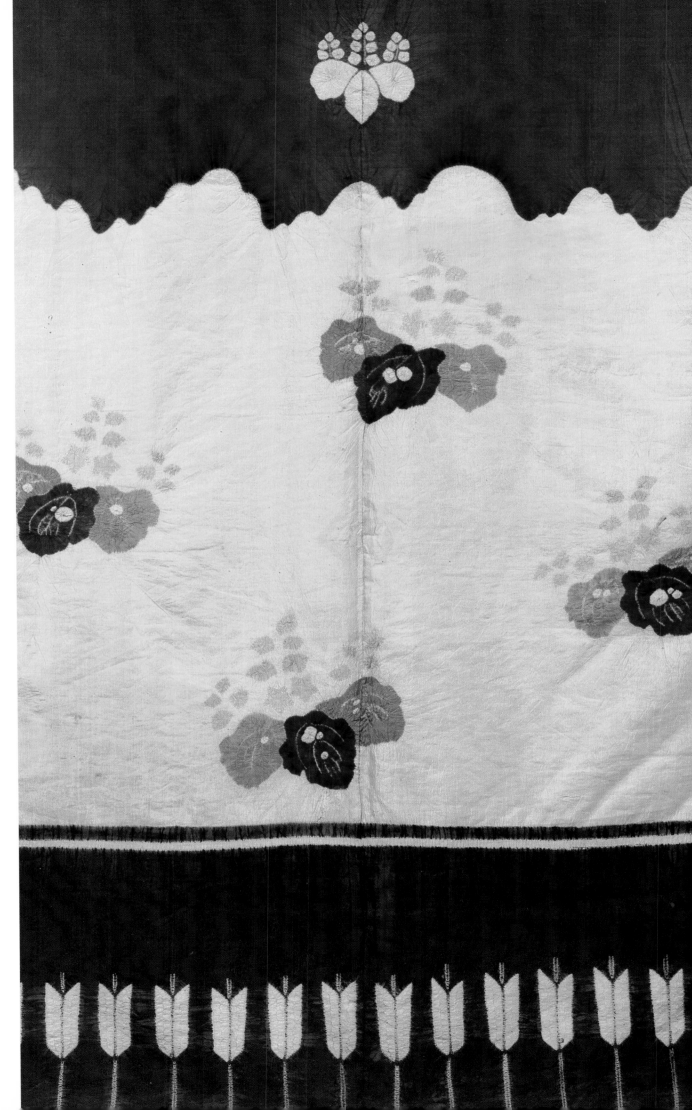

(Detail)

Cloth patterned by means of various resist dye techniques known collectively as *shibori* form the basis of the *tsujigahana* style of *kosode*. This *tsujigahana* garment is actually called a *dōbuku*, although it has the relatively narrow openings at the sleeve ends characteristic of a *kosode*. The *dōbuku* served as outer wear over armor and was frequently striking in appearance, in keeping with the fashion consciousness of the military men of that time. This example is thought to have once been a part of Toyotomi Hideyoshi's extensive wardrobe.

The paulownia motif was traditionally associated with the family of the empress. Here it is seen in a stylized form across the shoulders as a family crest (*mon*). It also appears in a more naturalistic rendering at the center of the robe. Along the hem is a line of feathered arrow shafts. The design format is based on the *kata-suso* arrangement, with the pattern and color concentrated at the shoulders and hem.

Latter half of the 16th century.

Pages 58-59 :

(Detail). An opulent, but perhaps overwrought effect is produced here by the profuse use of various *shibori* techniques, embroidery stitches, gold leaf and ink drawing.

Silk fabric, finely woven with small repeating motifs, replaced the plain weave *nerinuki* silk as the *kosode* fabric of choice early in the 17th century. In this example, *nerinuki* is still used, but the horizontal areas in white are patterned in gold leaf in imitation of figured silk.

The tiny embroidered motifs in the zigzag bands between the white areas, along with the *shibori*-dyed background color scheme of white, red and black, and the presence of motifs created by small spotted *shibori* dyeing are elements of the Keichō style, which followed as the next dominant fashion in *kosode*.

Early 18th century.

The *katabira* type of *kosode* was for summer wear and was not made of silk fabric as were all of the other *kosode* types. *Katabira* cloth was woven from ramie, a plant fiber. However, silk threads were always used for any embroidered motifs that appeared on these garments.

A combination of motifs that seem unrelated, but undoubtedly refer to a medieval literary work, appear in this delightfully asymmetric Kanbun for-

mat. A cosmetic box, a tasseled cord and fans are man-made objects that are juxtaposed with autumn flowers and crenulated roundels that symbolize snow flakes. The presence of autumn and winter motifs would have had a cooling psychological effect on the wearer and those who viewed the robe in the heat of summer.
Latter half of the 17th century.
Tokyo National Museum.

Mandarin ducks in water, giant waves that are edged with gold foam and green bamboo shoots form an enigmatic combination of motifs here. The curving triangular shape of the waves brings to mind sails and enhances the arching thrust of the design.

In their spareness and dynamism, Kanbun designs represent the *kosode* style that can most easily be appreciated by the modern viewer.
Latter half of the 17th century.
Tokyo National Museum.

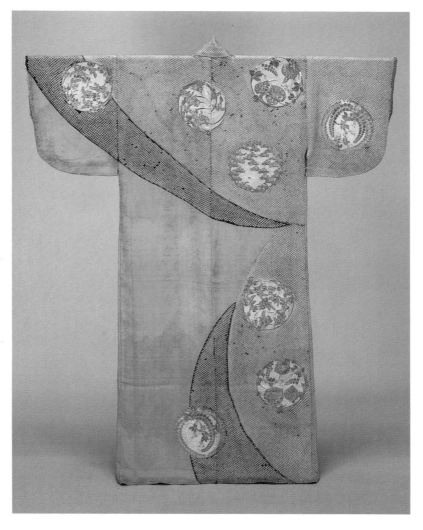

The waning influence of the Kanbun style can be seen here. Dyeing divides the surface of the *kosode* into color fields, as was more characteristic of earlier styles. The embroidered floral roundels tend to restrict the flow of the dyed pattern. Also, the embroidery itself is too detailed and used more gold thread than would normally be seen in a Kanbun *kosode*.

Roundels very similar to these were first published in a 1686 design book. If that was the source for these motifs, then this *kosode* was probably made around that date, which was several years after the end of the Kanbun era and just prior to the beginning of the Genroku era, which gave its name to the next major trend in *kosode* fashion.

Late 17th century.

Tokyo National Museum.

Written characters became a popular *kosode* motif during the latter half of the 17th century and usually allude to medieval literature. Here, the characters are rendered in spotted *shibori* and embroidered using gold and red silk threads. Their scale is varied, with the dyed characters appearing the largest. The surrounding stripes provide a dramatic contrast to the curvilinear characters.

Dyeing the multicolored stripes using the *shibori* method would have been a complicated process. Each of the four colors required a separate binding and dye immersion step. Complex techniques involving the use of dyes and pigments were developed during the second half of the 17th century, leading to the expansion of color and design possibilities in *kosode*.

Late 17th century.

Tokyo National Museum.

Above :
Peasant hats and maple leaves tinged with color denote an autumnal theme. The presence of the leaves makes for a more crowded composition, which counteracts any possible illusion created by the tilting hats, which would otherwise seem to be tumbling in the wind.

Rather than following the painstaking method of tying and dyeing to produce each of the spots that comprise the hats and leaves, a short cut method was employed involving the use of stencils. The presence of this technique and the denser patterning are elements of the Genroku style that would proliferate in later *kosode*.
Late 17th century.
Tokyo National Museum.

Right :
From the late 17th century onwards, the width of the *obi* increased adding to its importance as an element of dress. This also had an adverse effect on *kosode* design. For example, in this *kosode*, the plum blossoms and bamboo trellis appear evenly dispersed, with the undecorated area now almost crowded out of the design. This kind of composition became necessary because a more dynamic design would have been less effective if its midsection were covered by an *obi*. A solution to this problem was the use of continuous, overall design.

Another effect of the wider *obi* was to push motifs to the top and/or bottom of the *kosode*. Here, three written characters appear in gold thread embroidery across the top of the robe. They translate as " long live pleasure, " a fitting slogan for a garment that undoubtdly saw service in the licensed district.

This *katabira* uses the plum blossom as a reminder of cooler weather. It is the first flower of the year to bloom, appearing in late winter in Japan.
First half of the 18th century.
Tokyo National Museum.

Page 63 :
An evergreen is cleverly depicted here by its blossoms, which resemble chrysanthemums, and the wood grain pattern, looking somewhat like a stream, but probably meant as a reference to a tree trunk. Wisteria also appear intertwined amongst the other motifs.

The denser composition is typical of the Genroku style. The only undecorated areas of this *kosode* are at the left center of the body, across which the *obi* would be secured.
Late 17th/early 18th century.
Tokyo National Museum.

Richly decorated cloth partitions wrap around the front and back of the upper and lower portions of this *kosode*. Such curtains would be erected during outdoor events such as flower and leaf-viewing parties. The branches of colored maple leaves indicate that it is autumn.

A wide variety of floral and geometric patterns have been precisely rendered in *yūzen*, as have most of the maple leaves. For the remaining leaves and parts of the curtains, gold thread has been couched to the surface of the *chirimen* fabric. Three crests appear at the top of the robe, while two more are included on the front. Five repeated *mon* in this arrangement was the standard format from the 17th century onwards.

First half of the 19th century.
Tokyo National Museum.

Below and page 66 :
At its highest point of development, the *yūzen* technique allowed for pictorial designs that were as fully realized as those in paintings. Here, the principal motif of painted screens can be seen as a further emulation of the paint medium. Hawks and tasseled cords complete the imagery in this fluent arrangement based on the format of the Genroku style.
Purple blotches fill in much of the space between the motifs and were probably created by loosely bound resist dyeing. As is typical in *yūzen kosode*, embroidery is used sparingly, in this instance only for the cords and plum blossoms in the screens.
First half of the 18th century.
Tokyo National Museum.

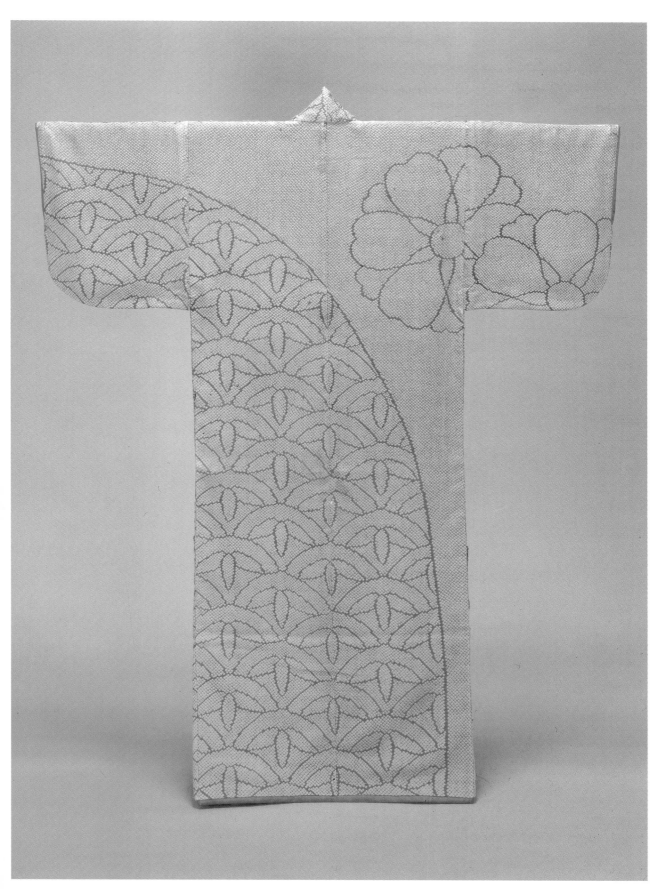

Spotted *shibori* dyeing is the sole means of patterning used for this *kosode*. The fabric is *rinzu*, the patterning of which is virtually nullified in this pointillistic rendering. Snow piled on bamboo leaves and cherry blossoms are symbolic of Winter and Spring.

Images derived from nature have always figured prominently in Japanese art and were meant to evoke a whole range of emotions and moods. This is not surprising in a country where Shinto, the only native religion, is based on a reverence for nature.

Latter half of the 17th century.
Tokyo National Museum.

(Detail)
Herons in a landscape dominated by water appear here as in the previous example. The addition of banks reinforced by basketry and a variety of vegetation make for a more image-laden scene that is reminiscent of *chayazome kosode* designs.

The literary allusions of *goshodoki* designs have much in common with those that appear in Nō theater costume. This was due to the fact that both the *goshodoki* style *kosode* and Nō costumes were made under samurai-class patronage. **First half of the 19th century.**
Tokyo National Museum.

(Detail)
Herons in aquatic settings are
another poetic theme illustrated
in samurai-class garments.
Nets, reeds, waves and spray
indicate the presence of a body
of water. As in many *goshodoki
kosode*, the motifs are rendered
in gold and silk thread embroidery and by means of resist
dyeing.

The crest are those of the
Tokugawa family, which was
actually a large clan with three
main branches. The shogun was
always a Tokugawa ; and the
clan was by far the wealthiest of
the daimyo families.

Crests were used by both the
chōnin and samurai families.
Townspeople devised numerous
crests that were used whim-
sically without regard to any
formal system of heraldry.
However, from the early 18th
century onwards, the lower
classes were prohibited from
using the three-ginger-leaf
Tokugawa crest.

First half of the 19th century.
Tokyo National Museum.

Left :
The combination of pine trees, bamboo and plum blossoms was considered highly auspicious. The three so-called " friends of winter " were also a symbol of perseverance because the pine and bamboo stayed green throughout the cold months and the plum blossoms opened in wintertime. Interspersed among these motifs are embroidered characters which allude to a medieval poem that expresses hope for a long and happy reign by the Emperor. The poem was adopted as the Japanese national anthem late in the 19th century.

Across the body of the robe at a point even with the bottom of the sleeves, a tuck was sewn to shorten the length of the garment. As with most *uchikake*, the hem has been thickly padded. The extra weight at the bottom helped to keep the unfastened garment from slipping off the shoulders. **Late 18th/early 19th century.**
Tokyo National Museum.

Right (detail) :
Another type of *kosode* favored by the samurai-class was the *uchikake*. It was worn draped over the shoulders like a cloak, unsecured by an *obi*.

This example has long semi-detached sleeves, which are characteristic of a type of *kosode* worn by young people called a *furisode*. *Furisode* were made of fabric in a variety of weaves, while *uchikake* almost always used *rinzu* as the ground fabric.

In this *uchikake*, plum blossoms, wild ginger leaves and chrysanthemums in a stream are rendered in *shibori* dyeing and embroidery on *rinzu*. **Late 18th/early 19th century.**
Tokyo National Museum.

Left :
Kosode in the *edozuma* style
reflect the exaggerated emphasis on the *obi* in Japanese dress.
Beginning in the latter half of
the 18th century, the *obi* was
approaching its greatest width
and most opulent appearance.
Kosode design formats that featured repeating motifs in symmetrical arrangements became
popular. These regular designs
were less likely to attract attention away from the *obi*.
Flower carts are evenly dispersed throughout this *kosode*,
which is of the *hitoe* type. This
motif was also common, in Nō
costumes. The carts' wheels are
wittily depicted in the form of
floral roundels. Butterflies,
clouds and decorative cords fill
in the remaining background
area. The front of the robe is
even more more densely patterned, as is characteristic of
the *edozuma* style.
Late 18th century.
Tokyo National Museum.

Below (detail) :
The flowers, leaves and buds
are rendered by either embroidery, ink drawing, or stencil
resist that imitates spotted
shibori. Technical variety helps
compensate for the somewhat
static design.
First half of the 19th century.
Tokyo National Museum.

Page 73 :
Another design format of the
edozuma style featured the
concentration of imagery along
the hem and lapels of the
kosode. It was both a reaction to
opulent overall designs and an
accomodation to the more
prominent *obi*.
Two auspicious themes are
presented here. The carp
swimming up the waterfall represents success in life. The
flowering tree at the left edge of
the garment is an evergreen, a
symbol of longevity.
Mid 19th century.
Tokyo National Museum.

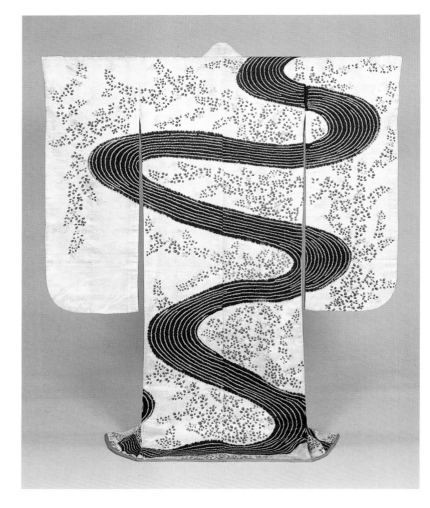

Because an *obi* was not worn with the *uchikake*, the garment's design was more fully seen. Here, bamboo blinds gracefully unfurl amidst flowering plum trees.

The unreal scale of the two motifs and the flowing arrangement of the blinds recall earlier *kosode* styles.

First half of the 19th century.

Bunka Gakuen Costume Museum, Tokyo.

The image of a stream meandering across every part of this robe presents an extreme example of the *kosode* as a flat surface that was made for the maximum expanse of artistic expression.

Bush clover is a melancholic autumnal motif more often seen on Nō costumes. Its presence is especially surprising alongside such an exuberantly rendered stream.

First half of the 19th century.

Kanebō Co., Ltd., Osaka.

(Detail)
A bamboo grove design is perfectly suited to the elongated *furisode* shape. A rhythmic interplay is created by the varied use of embroidery in gold thread and green silk, along with *shibori* spots, for the rendering of the bamboo stems and leaves.
First half of the 19th century.
Bunka Gakuen Costume Museum, Tokyo.

Right (Detail):
Countless spots produced by *shibori* dyeing form the clouds and bamboo motifs in this *furisode*-type *kosode*. In terms of textile technique, the robe is quite simple. However, laborious and precise binding was required to produce each spot in the design, making for an impressive example of workmanship. It is no wonder that this type of resist dyeing was periodically prohibited by the sumptuary laws.
Late 18th/early 19th century.
Tokyo National Museum.

Nō *Shōzoku*
Costumes
of the Nō Theater

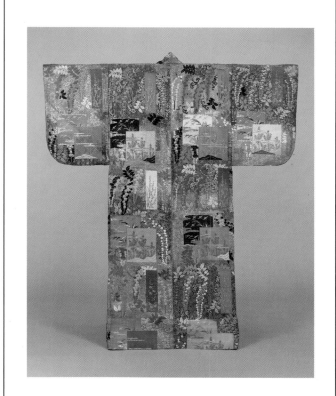

Pages 76-77 :
Repeat patterns are characteristic of woven cloth resulting from the mechanical nature of the loom. Extremely complicated motifs, including square and oblong painted sheets and wisteria are repeated here, and with each repetition, the motifs appear in a different color scheme. Adding to the complexity is a geometric star motif which appears throughout as a background pattern in *kinran* (gilt woven paper strips) and alternating background colors of red and brown. Only in Nishijin, the sophisticated weaving district of Kyoto, could a fabric as intricate as *karaori* be produced.
18th century.
Tokyo National Museum.

"I may be alone in thinking so, but to me it seems that nothing quite so becomes the Japanese skin as the costumes of the Nō theater. Of course many are gaudy in the extreme, richly woven of gold and silver... A robe woven or embroidered in patterns of gold or silver sets it [the skin] off beautifully, as does a cloak of deep green or persimmon"

In Praise of Shadows by Jun'ichirō Tanizaki (1886-1965)

(Detail)
A Nō performance is shown in what is probably a daimyo's residential compound. On the projecting stage in the center of the courtyard, a demon is attacking the other characters who are in a simple prop that represents a boat. Musicians and the chorus are seated at the near end of the stage. The most honored guests sit on either side of the stage. On one side are the men, who include two Buddhist clerics with shaved heads and barely visible *kesa*, along with other men in formal samurai garb. On the other side of the stage are upper-class women wearing *uchikake*. Some of the women are shielding their faces with fans.
40 × 103 ½ in.
(101.6 × 262.8 cm).
17th century screen painting.
Private collection, photo courtesy of Tiger Collection.

HISTORY OF NŌ THEATER

Nō as a theatrical form has been in existence for over six centuries and continues to be performed to this day. The word 'nō' can be translated as skill, accomplishment or talent.

Nō had its antecedents in *Dengaku*, performances based on Shinto agricultural rituals, and in *Sarugaku*, a popular form of entertainment combining mime, magic, comedy, songs and acrobatics. Zeami (1363-1443) and his father Kannami (1333-84) are considered to be the founders and

original theorists of Nō theater. Their status and the future of Nō was greatly enhanced by the patronage of shogun Ashikaga Yoshimitsu, who first saw the father and son team perform in 1374 at a shrine in Kyoto. With his support of Nō theater, Yoshimitsu provided the samurai class with a theatrical art to counter the various court forms of music and dance originally borrowed from China, including *Bugaku*, *Gigaku* and *Gagaku*.

Zeami wrote many plays that are ethereal in nature and share the Buddhist view of the transitory nature of life. The more worldly aspects of Nō's ancestry were retained in Kyōgen plays, staged as entertaining interludes between Nō plays. Ritualistic elements from the early beginnings of Nō were preserved in the special production called *Okina*, which preceded the presentation of Nō programs on certain occasions.

Zeami had little to say about the costuming of actors in his treatises on Nō. It is assumed that actors wore clothing donated by their samurai patrons, who awarded their own robes to honor and support the performing actors. An *ōsode* (wide sleeve opening) robe that belonged to shogun Ashikaga Yoshimasa (1436-90) is considered to be the earliest extant samurai garment that served as a Nō *shōzoku*.[1]

Support for Nō theater declined during the difficult *sengoku* period. Nō became reinvigorated in the sixteenth century as the result of Hideyoshi's enthusiastic support. Tokugawa Ieyasu realized the symbolic importance of Nō as a venerated samurai-class tradition. Various troupes of actors received the official backing of the shogunate and were given samurai status. Nō performances took place during state ceremonies including celebrations of the new year, elevations in the rank of important officials and investitures of shoguns.

The new official status of Nō required a more formal system of costuming to replace the donated samurai dress that was previously used. Consequently, the production of various types of Nō *shōzoku* specifically intended for use on stage began under the patronage of Hideyoshi and Ieyasu.

ELEMENTS AND PRINCIPLES OF NŌ THEATER

The basic theatrical elements of Nō, such as setting, character and plot, are quite simple in comparison to traditional Western theater. Nō was staged outdoors until the late nineteenth century. A roof covered the stage, providing protection from the elements and symbolically delineating a sacred performance space. Lighting was provided by torches for evening performances, or plays were otherwise presented in daylight. No curtain separated the audience from the bare wooden stage. There were no sets ; a painting of a pine tree and bamboo served as a backdrop. A minimum of propos appeared on the stage. The vivid costumes essentially served as scenery in motion.

The scene illustrated here appears to be from the Nō play *Kurozuka*. The main character is an old woman turned demoness, who attacks a Buddhist cleric (shown in the foreground and identifiable by the Buddhist swastika near the hilt of his sword) and his companion. They have come to seek shelter in her rustic hut, represented by the prop in the background. The actor playing the old woman/demoness wears a *surihaku* under robe, decorated with metallic foil in the so-called "fish scale" pattern, which denotes the non-human aspects of the character. By allowing the outer robe to fall off the shoulders and drape around the waist, the underrobe is revealed, signaling the transformation of the character into a demoness. The outer robe is a *nuihaku*-type Nō costume decorated with metallic foil and embroidery in a pattern of scattered *mon*.

All roles have always been played by adult male actors and young boys, who perform both child and adult roles. Few actors appeared on stage at the same time. Often just the main character (*shite*) and the supporting character (*waki*) are present. *Shite* roles tend to be other-worldly, featuring gods, demons and ghosts, but can also include tragic historical figures and the insane. The character might be either male or female. The *shite* usually wears a mask and moves in a deliberate and stylized manner while chanting his lines. *Waki* actors always play men who inhabit the world of the living such as Buddhist clerics, shrine attendants, samurai or farmers. On stage the *waki* is unmasked and relatively passive in comparison to the *shite*. Music and song are provided by musicians playing flutes and drums and a chanting chorus, who sit Japanese-style on the stage. They complement and help advance the actions of the actors.

Plots of Nō plays are minimal and are based on well-known stories taken mostly from the medieval past. Events from myths, legends, poetry and novels such as *Genji Monogatari* (*Tales of Genji*, written in the eleventh century) are the sources for many of the plots. The plays that are still performed today number just over two hundred out of a total of more than three thousand that were written during the course of Nō's history.

Much has been written about the aesthetics of Nō by Zeami and other theorists since his time. Terms that describe what is meant to be expressed

A scene from *Dōjō-ji*, a play about a young woman who falls in love with a Buddhist cleric. Her desire turns her into a demoness. The character has a demon mask and wears a lined *kariginu*-type Nō robe over an *atsuita* inner robe, a combination that is suitable for such a role. The voluminous trousers (*hakama*) are of a type known as *hangire*, and are also appropriate for demon roles. The prop is meant to denote a bronze temple bell.
16 in. high (40.5 cm).
Detail from a handscroll by Sesshin Fukuo (1716-85)
Spencer Collection, The New York Public Library. Astor, Lenox and Tilden Foundations.

and felt in a Nō performance include *hana, yūgen* and *rojaku.*[2] None of these terms are easily definable and their meanings have changed over time, but for the purpose of providing a glimpse into the subtlety of Nō, they can be defined as follows. *Hana* refers to the visual beauty of the performance and the 'inner' beauty that the actors express on stage. *Yūgen* (literally "profound sublimity") is a subjective quality of elegance and grace that is also part of the aesthetic vocabulary of poetry and the tea ceremony. *Rojaku* represents the awareness and sadness that comes at the end of a lifetime understanding of reality and illusion.

NŌ THEATER AND THE SAMURAI CLASS

Under the Tokugawa rule, one of the many duties of daimyo was to uphold the samurai tradition of Nō theater. The ability to give an impromptu rendition of a Nō role was an important measure of cultivation amongst daimyo. Nō *shōzoku* were among the *omote dogu* (official articles) required in a proper daimyo household. Due to the custom of preserving family valuables that was practiced by upper-echelon samurai, a very large number of Nō costumes are extant. In just one of the Tokugawa clan's three branches, approximately six hundred *shōzoku* dating from the seventeenth to the mid-nineteenth century have been maintained to the present day.[3] In collections both inside and outside Japan Nō robes of this period far outnumber contemporary *kosode.*

In the theatrical arts of the period, Nō theater was to the samurai class what Kabuki theater was to the *chōnin* class. An example of the difference between the two performing arts can be seen in the varying styles of the *onnagata.* In Kabuki, the *onnagata* impersonated a woman, whereas in Nō the idea was to capture the essence of a woman.[4] The kabuki *onnagata* were admired as celebrities and often started fashion trends, unlike their more private Nō counterparts. Ukiyoe prints, being a *chōnin* art form, rarely depicted Nō performances or actors, however, Kabuki actors and performances were a favored subject for the woodblock prints.

As mentioned in Chapter 1, in contrast to the townspeople, the economic fortunes of the samurai class declined during the Tokugawa rule. Nō troupes were allowed to hold public fund-raising performances when daimyo support lagged during periods of austerity. The indignities faced by the performers from the presence of rowdy lower-class audiences must have been a painful reminder of the general decline of the samurai class.

KOSODE AND NŌ *SHŌZOKU*

Nō *shōzoku* are more representative of pre-seventeenth century upper-class dress traditions than the changing *kosode* styles of the mid-sixteenth through mid-nineteenth centuries. However, due in part to the requirements of stage costuming and their exemption from sumptuary laws, Nō *shozōku* displayed vitality and creativity. The need to project visually from a stage, often under dim lighting, resulted in the production of many bold, coloful and heavily gilded Nō costumes. Competition among daimyo, untempered by sumptuary laws, created a demand for clever and striking costumes that was met by the flourishing textile industry based in the Nishijin district of Kyoto.

Woven patterning is the principal means of decoration found on most types of Nō costumes, as it was on the donated upper-class garments worn by actors in the early centuries of Nō. Whereas new dyeing techniques were an important part of changing *kosode* styles, pattern dyeing as practiced in *kosode* was generally avoided by the makers of Nō robes, probably because of the lower-class associations of most of those dyeing techniques. Pattern dyeing was, however, the standard means of decoration for the costumes used in Kyōgen plays, which featured lower-class characters in comic situations in contrast to the somber Nō plays.

A type of pattern dyeing which does appear in various kinds of Nō costumes is warp ikat, which involves the resist dyeing of individual warp threads in order to produce a color change. This kind of dyeing is not found on *kosode* until the late nineteenth century, but was a feature of some pre-seventeenth century upper-class clothing.[5] In Nō robes, warp ikat dyeing is usually present in combination with woven motifs.

Nō costumes were generally unaffected by the changing design formats of *kosode*, and consequently are not as easy to place chronologically. The lack of stylistic change is not surprising in light of the traditional nature of Nō theater. Also, unlike *kosode*, the width of the *obi* used for Nō costumes remained narrow and unchanging, thereby removing that element as a stylistic influence. Another factor that contributed to the constancy of *shōzoku* design concerns the nature of woven patterns. The pattern repeats common in weaving make asymmetrical formats, such as those appearing in *kosode*, highly impractical.

In spite of these factors, Nō robes have individual characters. It is unusual to find two that are identical. As in *kosode*, the component parts of the finished robe originated from a single narrow bolt of cloth, decorated according to a pre-determined layout that resulted in a completed, fully realized design when cut into component panels, juxtaposed, and sewn. One means of varying the appearance of woven *shōzoku* was to align the panels of fabric creatively in the cutting and sewing of the robes. Another way in which interesting designs were created was by varying the subject, size, spacing and coloration of individual motifs.

Kosode and Nō costumes also differed in the motifs used. Buddhist symbols, such as the lotus, *rimbō* (a wheel signifying the Buddhist law) and

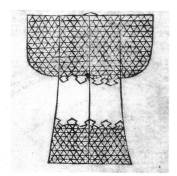

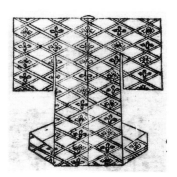

umban (cloud-shaped gong used in Buddhist monasteries) were common in Nō robes, but nonexistent as *kosode* motifs. Motifs based on everyday objects did occasionally appear in *shōzoku*, although less frequently than in *kosode*.

A similarity that did exist between the two forms of dress was in the manner in which upper-class garments were traditionally worn. Nō costumes were worn in layers, in the same way that samurai wore certain types of *kosode* together, such as the *koshimaki* over a *katabira* or a *hitoe*, and the *uchikake* over a *kosode* or a *furisode*.

Two pages from a Nō theater manual. The types of costumes illustrated from top to bottom are a *surihaku* (but at that time called a *shirohaku*), an *atsuita*, a *happi* and a *kariginu*; however, the body of the latter costume is depicted as comprising two widths of cloth instead of the usual single width that is customary for this kind of costume. Such manuals were used to familiarize performers and connoisseurs with all aspects of the Nō performance.
11 × 8 ¾ in. (28 × 22 cm).
Woodblock printed book entitled Nō no zushiki (1697).
Spencer Collection, The New York Public Library. Astor, Lenox and Tilden Foundations.

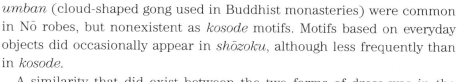

TYPES OF NŌ *SHŌZOKU*

Nō robes can be divided into two broad categories, those having *kosode*-type narrow sleeve openings, and those with the wide sleeve openings of the *ōsode*. The Nō costumes with the *kosode*-like sleeves will be discussed first.

Nuihaku

The *nuihaku* Nō costumes were literally interchangeable with *nuihaku kosode* up until the seventeenth century, since they were donated to Nō troupes after being worn by samurai. *Nuihaku* then declined as a *kosode* style when this type of Nō robe was first made expressly for use as a stage costume.

In *kosode*, the pattern-dyeing of *tsujigahana* had merged with *nuihaku*, leading to the subsequent Keichō style. Patterned *rinzu* had replaced plain-woven unpatterned *nerinuki* as the favored *kosode* fabric. Although *nuihaku* Nō robes were pattern-dyed, this process was used to obtain checkered and striped multicolored backgrounds, instead of the figured and abstract motifs of *kosode*. *Rinzu* was used as a ground fabric in *nuihaku shōzoku*, but unpatterned fabrics were also used, in keeping with the earlier usage of plain-woven materials for *nuihaku* garments. Like *kosode*, *nuihaku* costumes also changed their shape, becoming wider in the sleeves and narrower in the body and lapels.

The primary *nuihaku* techniques, combining embroidery with glued-on gold or silver leaf, were maintained as the method of decorating *nuihaku* costumes, making this one of the rare *shōzoku* with non-woven patterning.

The *nuihaku kosode* formats of the sixteenth century were not always continued in later Nō robes. However, the stage costumes followed symmetrical design formats, as opposed to the asymmetrical trend in *kosode* design.

Nuihaku were mostly worn for female roles, often over a *surihaku* costume. The manner in which the *nuihaku* was usually worn is called *koshimaki*, meaning the robe does not cover the shoulders, but is draped around the waist. *Nuihaku* costumes were also specially made for children's roles.

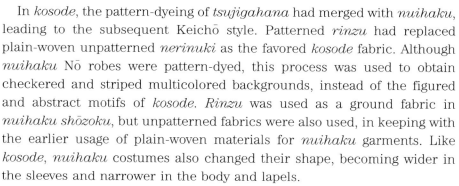

Stripes, a gilded wood grain pattern, embroidered snow flake medallions and bamboo leaves are repeated throughout this *nuihaku*. Since all of the motifs continually span the various seams of the garment, a prodigious effort was required in decorating the single fabric length from which this robe was made. The fact that some of the repeating motifs are slightly off register at a seam is certainly to be excused in a robe with such a design.
19th century.
Bunka Gakuen Costume Museum, Tokyo.

Surihaku

The *surihaku* is an under-robe for female roles, patterned only by means of metallic foil and glue applied by stencils, usually on white silk. Gold foil appears in costumes for young women, and silver is used for older women's roles.

Karaori

Karaori shōzoku are the most elaborate of the Nō robes, with *kosode*-type sleeves. *Karaori* (literally "Chinese weave") was a woven fabric originally made in China. In Nō costume, it often incorporates warps of raw silk that

A white, pale blue and green checkered background is unusual for a *surihaku shōzoku*. This kind of design format is called *dan gawari* and is found in several types of Nō costumes. A zigzag pattern, imaginatively named "mountain path" has been applied in silver leaf. The use of silver on white indicates an older woman's role.
19th century.
Bunka Gakuen Costume Museum, Tokyo.

can be ikat patterned, in combination with long floating wefts of degummed silk, and gilt or silvered strips of paper (*kinran* and *ginran* respectively), also used as wefts. This weave often resulted in complex designs featuring pattern on several visual levels. The bottommost layer of pattern might be ikat-dyed, producing blurred edges on areas of color or distinct blocks of changing background color. The next visual level was often a repeat geometric pattern rendered by the metallic strips. Long floating wefts resembling embroidery usually appeared outermost, forming large-scale figural motifs.

Karaori were worn primarily for female roles over a *nuihaku* or *surihaku*. There were varied ways of wearing *karaori* costumes, including around the waist (*koshimaki*), with the right arm out of the sleeve (*nugi-sage*) or with the hem of the robe lifted up and tucked into the trouser-like *hakama* (*tsubo-ori*). These modes were based on the manner of wearing *kasaori kosode* once prevalent amongst upper-class women. The *karaori kosode* went out of fashion in the seventeenth century but, like the *nuihaku kosode*, took on a new life as a Nō costume.[6]

Worn out *karaori* costumes were remodelled for children's roles. The sleeves were made long and semi-detached, as in *kosode* with 'swinging sleeves' worn by young people. *Karaori* with red coloration were worn for youthful roles, and those without were for middle-aged or elderly roles. Robes with red colors and 'swinging sleeves' were reserved for the youngest characters.

(Detail)
The *karaori* type of Nō costume was based on earlier upper-class dress, as was the *nuihaku*. From the 17th century onwards, *kosode* in the complicated *karaori* weave were no longer fashionable, but some of the most opulent Nō *shōzoku* continued to be made of *karaori* fabric.
Cherry trees, buds and flowers appear in the undyed blocks. The tree trunks are shown out of scale and equal in size to the flowers. Exposure of the trees' roots was a convention borrowed from Chinese art. The red blocks feature the imperial symbols of the stylized chrysanthemum and paulownia on a zigzag pattern.
Latter half of the 16th century.
Tokyo National Museum.

Four actors wearing masks, playing young women's roles appear as the attendants of the character inside the carriage. The outer robes of the attendants appear to be the *karaori* type worn for young female roles. The outer robe of the performer in the carriage, also probably a *karaori*, is worn gathered up in front, revealing voluminous trousers called *ōkuchi*. The combination of garments and the manner in which they are worn, indicate a court lady.
16 in. high (40.5 cm).
Detail from a handscroll by Sesshin Fukuo (1716-85).
Spencer Collection, The New York Public Library. Astor, Lenox and Tilden Foundations.

(Detail)
Used principally as an inner robe, for male roles the *atsuita* Nō costume tended to be bolder and less complex in design than the *karaori*. A paired water wheel motif is featured here, along with an ancient geometric pattern of hexagons enclosing stylized flowers.

This type of water wheel was a popular motif in 16th and 17th century Japanese art. It often appeared in traditional compositions showing a famous bridge over the Uji River near Kyoto. The depiction of the water wheel was an allusion to that scene. Because Uji has a sound that is similar to the Japanese word for gloom, the motif evokes a mood that was appropriate for the Nō theater.

Sections from another garment were added to this robe in order to lenghten it ; and the sleeves were later remade in accordance with the post-16th century manner.
Latter half of the 16th century.
Tokyo National Museum.

Atsuita

The *atsuita shōzoku* shares the basic technical features of the *karaori*, but its weft float motifs are fewer and have shorter spans, giving the costume a flatter appearance. The designs are generally bolder than those seen in *karaori* robes. The term *atsuita* is derived from the word for the thick boards over which bolts of heavy imported cloth were wrapped in earlier times. *Atsuita* costumes usually signified male characters and were generally worn as an inner robe in combination with one of several types of *ōsode* robes.

Atsuita karaori

A category of Nō *shōzoku* which has become increasingly indistinct since the mid-nineteenth century was called *atsuita karaori*. It combined the features of both of those robes and served as either an inner or outer robe, usually for male characters.

This lion-like beast (often mistakenly called a dog) originally came to Japan from China as a Buddhist symbol. It served as the mount for the Buddhist deity called Monju in Japanese. In later times it was usually depicted with the peony in what was considered an auspicious combination.

The dating of Nō costumes is often a matter of educated guesswork. Motifs, techniques, materials and compositions did not change significantly over time as they did with *kosode*. In the absence of historical records, one of the best chronological clues, is in the aging of the silk, dyes and metallic paper strips used in the robe.
18th century.
Tokyo National Museum.

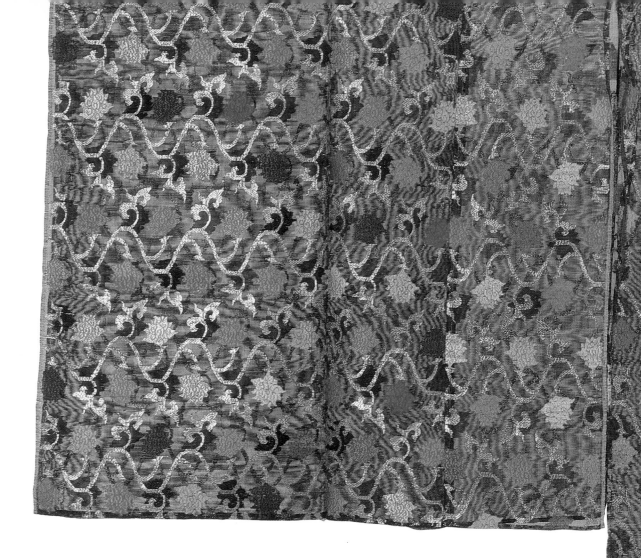

Noshime

The final type of Nō robe with the *kosode* sleeve is the *noshime* worn by male characters usually as an inner robe under any one of several of the *ōsode*-type costumes. In design and weave, it is the least complex of the *kosode*-sleeved *shōzoku*. *Noshime* either contain geometric designs or are undecorated, and are always in a plain weave. In keeping with its simplicity, this type of costume often denoted a low-ranking samurai, a farmer or an elderly person, and was also worn by actors in Kyōgen plays.

Ōsode Nō *shōzoku*

Osode were the outer garments of the medieval nobility, featuring unsewn sleeve ends and a sleeve width that was very broad in the horizontal direction. Nō costumes with *ōsode*-type sleeves are all weave-patterned, in keeping with *ōsode* worn by the upper classes in earlier times. An exception is the *suō*, which is made of resist-dyed hemp, and worn by actors performing roles of commoners in both Nō and Kyōgen plays. Another resist-dyed hemp costume, the *hitatare*, was used primarily in *Okina*, the symbolic prelude to special Nō programs.

The *kariginu*, modelled after a traditional court garment, has a high round collar, a long narrow body unsewn at the sides, and cords held in place by loops attached to the sleeve ends. Lined *kariginu* are made of

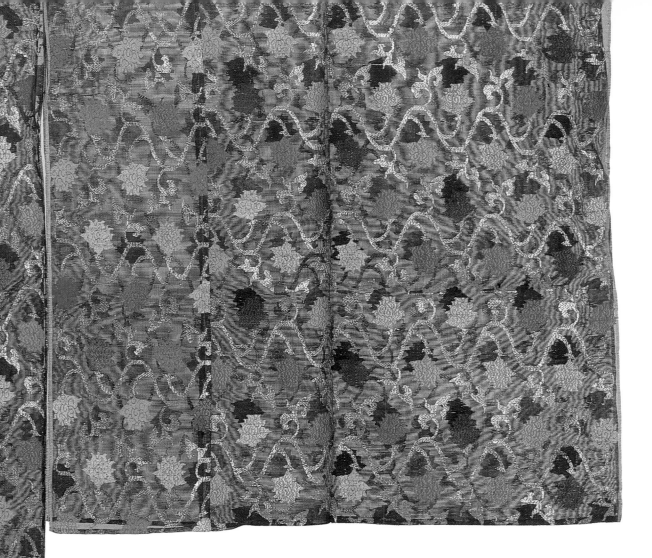

fabric in any of several compound weaves that usually include flat metallic strips (*kinran* or *ginran*). Actors wearing this costume often played supernatural roles. Unlined *kariginu* are made of gauze patterned with *kinran* and are used primarily to denote a high-ranking noble. The absence of a lining on a gauze-woven robe adds to the diaphanous appearance of the gauze. The *nōshi*, a costume very similar to the unlined *kariginu*, denoted the highest ranking aristocrats.

A short-bodied *shōzoku*, open at the sides, with fabric tabs joining the front and back panels of the robe, is known as the *happi*. It is made of similar fabrics to those used for *kariginu* and is meant ot represent armor worn by medieval military leaders. The sleeveless version of this costume, called *sobatsugi*, designated lower-ranking warriors.

The three remaining types of *ōsode shōzuku* are usually of gauze-weave and unlined. They are particularly favored for roles which require dance movements ; and the costumes seem to have been developed for the stage, rather than being based on medieval garments. *Chōken* are open at the sides, relatively short-bodied, and are fastened by long cords, attached to the front panels of the robe. *Kinran* and polychrome silk threads usually provide the patterning in this costume used primarily for female roles. The *maiginu* is similar to the *chōken*, except that its body panels are sewn at the sides and it has no fastening cords. Lastly, the *mizugoromo* has sleeves that are narrower in the vertical direction and is more simply patterned than the *chōken* or the *maiginu*.

The other principal category of Nō *shozoku* consists of costumes with *ōsode*-type sleeves. Unlike the narrow openings at the ends of the *kosode*-type sleeve, the openings at the sleeve ends were left unsewn. Each sleeve of the *ōsode* costume is as wide or wider than the body of the robe. Most of these were derived from medieval upper-class outer garments, which in turn were based on Chinese dress. These costumes therefore tend to be conservative in terms of color and composition.

This *kariginu* costume is decorated with a peony motif in the ancient Chinese scrolling vine pattern. In China and Japan, the peony was considered as a symbol of nobility and therefore an appropriate motif on a *kariginu*, worn for aristocratic roles. This example is unlined, and made of a gauze and *kinran* fabric. The cords that were usually attached to the sleeve ends are missing.

18th century.
Tokyo National Museum.

NŌ *SHŌZOKU* AS USED IN PERFORMANCES

Whereas the spoken lines of a Nō play follow a particular script, the music, stage movements, and choices of masks and costumes are not specified. In regard to costumes, factors that influence the choice of robes include the role to be played, the customs of the troupe to which the actor belongs, and the mood of the actor. Conditions such as the season, time and circumstance of the performance further affect the costume selections. The colors, designs and technical characteristics for each combination of *shōzoku* required by a particular role take the above factors into consideration.

Masks represent another variable that is important in costuming. A role in a play can be performed using a variety of different combinations of masks and costumes, including variations as to how the costumes are worn, such as *koshimaki* or *nugisage*.[7] A specific combination of robes, for example a *karaori* over a *nuihaku*, could be worn with different masks to represent a different character in various plays, although the characters would be of the same general type, such as supernatural beings. A specific kind of mask, in combination with different sets of costumes worn in varying ways, could represent different characters, although these characters might be of various types, such as the ghost of a princess, a courtesan or a poet.[8]

NOTES

1. Seiroku Noma, *Japanese Costume and Textile Arts*, trans. by Armins Nikovski, New York, Weatherhill/Heibonsha, 1977, pp. 54, 55, pls. 46, 94.

2. Kunio Komparu, *The Noh Theater : Principles and Perspectives*, trans. by Jane Corddry, New York, John Weatherhill, Inc., 1983, pp. 10-15.

3. Sadao Ōkochi and Yoshinobu Tokugawa, *The Tokugawa Collection : Nō Robes and Masks*, trans. by Monica Bethe and Louise Allison Cort, New York, Japan Society, 1977, p. 22.

4. Komparu, op. cit., pp. 51, 52.

5. Mary Dusenbury, "Kasuri : A Japanese Textile", *Textile Museum Journal*, vol. 17, 1978, pp. 44, 45.

6. Ōkochi and Tokugawa, op. cit., p. 19.

7. Komparu, op. cit., pp. 298-99.

8. Komparu, op. cit., p. 297.

Right (detail) :
Medieval ox-drawn court carriages dominate the left half of this *nuihaku*, while lilies cover most of the right half. Each of the two motifs elegantly intermingle across the seam that joins the body panels. Throughout the robe, vertical wavy lines composed of a key fret pattern in gold leaf create a sense of depth in the overall design by appearing to be underneath the embroidered carriages and flowers. The wildly outscaled proportions of the lilies in relation to the carriages add a further touch of illusion to the costume.

The lily entered the Japanese design repertory with the coming of the Europeans in the 16th century. It fell out of favor by the middle of the next century with the expulsion of foreigners and the banning of Christianity.

Latter half of the 16th century.
Tokyo National Museum.

Plates

Page 94 :
The *nuihaku* Nō costume continued the tradition of the upper-class *nuihaku kosode*, which had been one type of garment from daimyo wardrobes that was previously bestowed upon Nō actors in recognition of a fine performance. This robe belonged to an important daimyo family and was made during the second half of the 16th century, when Nō costume production was initiated and *shōzoku* were made expressly for use on the stage.

The characteristic *nuihaku* techniques of embroidery and applied metallic foil are used profusely on a changing color ground in this example. Multicolored backgrounds in stripes or blocks are seen on several types of Nō costumes. One technique used for producing this effect was *shibori* dyeing, a method that was more commonly employed for patterning *kosode*. Two other ways of making the parti-colored backgrounds were unique to Nō costume production. One was the ikat technique, which involved the resist dyeing of threads, rather than whole cloth. The other method consisted of a patterned weave wherein the changing colors were the result of woven polychrome weft. In this *nuihaku* a combination of the latter two techniques was used to create the alternating white and reddish orange background.

A front view of the costume is shown here, and the back is similarly decorated, as with virtually all Nō robes. The various motifs include chrysanthemums, grasses, snow-covered willows and sea shells, among the images from nature, along with two man-made objects, a plank bridge and streamers in the form of long strips of papers used for painting and writing poetry.
Latter half of the 16th century.
Tokyo National Museum.

A pair of mandarin ducks amidst water plants appear on alternate blocks of the body of this costume. Gold and silver foil fill in the narrow spaces between the densely packed embroidery. Chrysanthemums and grassy mounds are embroidered on the blocks that are dyed reddish orange. The plain-woven *nerinuki* fabric that was often used for 16th century *kosode* also serves as the ground cloth in this example.

When new, the robe would have appeared even more opulent than it does now. The silver foil has tarnished, much of the gold foil has disappeared, and the dyes, especially the reddish orange, have faded. Also, the alternating pattern would have continued from the body to the sleeves had the garment not been retailored.

During the Tokugawa rule, Nō actors were given samurai status, and several of the all-male troupes were officially sanctioned by the government. This robe belonged to the Komparu family, who headed one of the established schools of Nō theater, as they continue to do to this day.

Latter half of the 16th century.

Tokyo National Museum.

Autumn has always been the season that evoked the most poignant expressions in Japanese art and literature. *Akikusa*, a traditional grouping of seven flowers and plants associated with the fall, are a frequentlyused source of motifs in Nō robes.

The flower carts contain bush clover, Chinese bellflower, pampas grass (*L. Miscanthus*), and "maiden flower" (*L. Valerian or Patrina*) from among the *akikusa* set of motifs. Another fall flower, the chrysanthemum, originally a symbol of longevity in China and identified with the emperor in Japan, also appears, along with iris, which is customarily associated with summer. Butterflies complete the embroidered images, which are worked on fabric completely covered with gold leaf.

18th century.

Tokyo National Museum.

Page 97 :

An agricultural theme in embroidery with sickles, horsetails and bundled horsetails used for scouring, decorates the top of the robe, and flowering plants with a bamboo fence are shown below. The arrangement of motifs concentrated at the shoulders and hem was also seen in *kosode*. Such a design format would seem to be a practical choice for a stage costume which was only partially exposed, often only at the top or bottom. However, the *kata suso* format was infrequently used on *nuihaku* after the 16th century. An agricultural theme is appropriate on a costume made for the Nō theater, as Nō was based, in part, on Dengaku, a performance art that was included in Shinto agricultural rites.

A weave-patterned silk serves as the ground fabric here, as it does in most *kosode*. An unusual abstract pattern in gold leaf is applied to the fabric. Within the zigzag lines at the center of the robe, a dew-laden grass motif has also been applied in gold leaf.

18th century.

Tokyo National Museum.

(Detail). This *nuihaku* has embroidery on a yellow satin-weave silk, creating an effect similar to the previous example with its gilded background. The fabric is actually patterned with tiny scale motifs of sails, mist and pine branches in gold leaf, however, they are barely visible on the yellow satin. The use of the poppy as the principal motif is unusual in Japanese art.

In spite of the lush materials and intricate workmanship that went into the making of *nuihaku* Nō costumes, this type of robe was often obscured from view during performances. It was usually worn off the shoulders and draped around the waist over another costume such as the *surihaku*. It could also serve as an inner robe, in which case even less of the garment was seen.

18th century.

Tokyo National Museum.

(Detail)

The *surihaku* type of Nō robe is the simplest of the stage costumes in the *kosode*-sleeve category, as far as technique and design are concerned. Usually, the *surihaku* is patterned by means of metallic foil applied to white satin-weave silk. Its use is more restricted than the other *shōzoku* of this category, since *surihaku* are always worn as an under robe for female roles.

The use of gold foil rather than silver, and the presence of red coloring, indicates that this costume was intended for a young female role. The robe is short in the body and has relatively long semi-detached sleeves associated with a *furisode*, which further indicates its having been used for a youthful role.

The grapevine was a popular motif during the 16th century, and here it is shown in combination with decorated square sheets of paper used for painting and writing poetry. This robe also has the sleeve and body proportions which are characteristic of 16th century garments.

Latter half of the 16th century.

Tokyo National Museum.

(Detail)
The ephemeral nature of dew made it a fitting image for a Nō costume. The grass, which is bent over by the weight of the dew, is rendered in gold and silver (now tarnished) leaf.

A white background indicates that this costume was meant for an older woman's role. Only the top half of the robe would have been seen when the outer robe was worn off the shoulders. Even so, the dense dew-laden grass pattern is ended with a carefully executed " pine bark " pattern and there are a few scattered blades of grass and dew drops that were applied below that motif, which would also have gone unseen during a performance. The unseen and the implied were important aspects that contributed to the subtlety of Nō theater.

18th century.

Tokyo National Museum.

Pages 100-101 (detail) :
Autumnal motifs abound here, and include the carnation, bush clover and Chinese bellflower from the *akikusa* grouping, and also maple leaves and chrysanthemums. The long floating wefts, which are characteristic of the *karaori* weave, give a greater physical presence to those motifs. The bamboo fence, dew-laden grass and stylized wave motifs are depicted primarily in *kinran* and appear as a background pattern in the total design scheme. Changing blocks of color created by ikat dyeing add another layer of pattern to the costume. *Karaori* serve as outer robes for female roles. The substantial amount of red in this robe's color scheme indicate that it would have been used for the role of a younger woman.

18th century.

Tokyo National Museum.

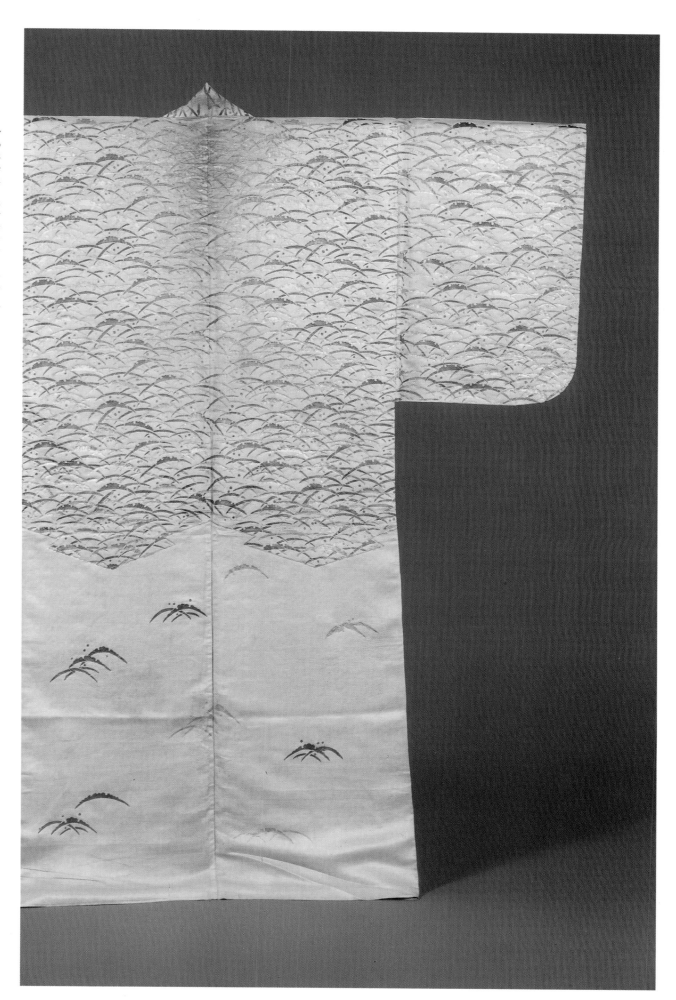

(Detail)
A relatively simple design of wisteria on a grid of interlocking circles. Even in this more basic layout, the color scheme is varied in each of the wisteria blossom repeats.

A design with large-scale images such as these would have a more direct visual impact on stage. However, this *karaori* also has a subtle aspect. The interlocking circles are woven in *kinran*, which almost disappears on the yellow silk ground. This pattern would only have been seen as a fleeting glimmer of gold in the low light of a Nō performance.

18th century.
Tokyo National Museum.

The Nō theater was the performing art of the samurai class, just as Kabuki theater was identified with the lower classes. The economic well-being of the samurai had declined by the 19th century, much to the detriment of the Nō theater and its costumes.

This late *karaori*, with its repeating colors and pattern of bush clover, seems stiff and ordinary in comparison with earlier examples.

19th century.

Bunka Gakuen Costume Museum, Tokyo.

Page 104 :
Scattered Chinese and Japanese written characters appear in both Nō robes and *kosode*, always as an allusion to earlier literature that served as the source for many of the plots of Nō plays.

The striking design format of differing halves (*katami gawari*) is one of the older divided garment formats adopted by Nō costume designers, along with *kata suso* and the checkerboard layout (*dan gawari*).

Kinran is used extensively here in an interesting reciprocal manner. The characters appear in silk against a *kinran* ground on the right half of the robe, with the relationship in reverse on the left half.

17th century.

Tokyo National Museum.

Page 105 :
Green flowering bush clover
on a brown ground is barely
visible in the darker blocks.
Bush clover flowers very
briefly with delicate blossoms that are quickly de-
stroyed by wind and rain,
making them a fitting symbol
for the transience of beauty
and life. Bamboo, the other
major motif on this *atsuita*
costume, is admired for its
steadfastness because it
bends, but does not break.
The transitions between
blocks are hazy rather than
sharply defined. This is the
result of deliberate shifting
of the warp threads after they
has been dyed by means of
the ikat process.
18th century.
Tokyo National Museum.

(Detail)
The wavy line pattern e
closes paulownia and s
lized floral lozenges. T
color schemes are varied
each motif is repeated.
Repairs have been made
this costume during t
course of its existence, a
at some point it w
retailored for a child's ro
Most Nō costumes were us
repeatedly over a long peri
of time. Abrasion result
from the actor's movemen
the wearing of multiple rob
and the use of a sash to ke
the costumes in place. S
and metallic paper stri
become brittle over time a
certain dyes and mordar
corrode silk threads. Final
fabrics with special featur
such as *karaori*, with
long, raised floating wef
and *atsuita*, with its st
weave, are especially susce
tible to wear. Remaking
adult robe into one suitab
for a child's role was a pra
tical way of saving ar
reusing these valuable cc
tumes.
17th century.
Tokyo National Museum.

(Detail)

This is a somewhat complicated design for an *atsuita*.
The background colors
change, as do the patterns,
alternating between triangles
and clouds. The figural motifs, which are repeated in
changing color schemes, include a dragon in a lozenge
shape, part of a wheel and a
stylized flower.

In medieval times, wooden
wheels were periodically
soaked in water to prevent
them from cracking. When
in use, they were attached to
ox-driven court carriages.
Therefore, the half-
submerged wheel serves as
an abbreviated symbol for
the courtly life in medieval
times, an important source
of subject matter for the Nō
theater.

18th century.

Tokyo National Museum.

Color, rather than color and pattern, dominates this *atsuita*. It serves to enliven the traditional paired crane motif repeated throughout the costume. Had the fabric been in a plain weave, instead of a figured weave, the costume would have been considered a typical example of the *noshime* type of Nō *shōzoku*. **19th century.**
Bunka Gakuen Costume Museum, Tokyo.

Pages 110-111 :
(Detail). The clematis is a summer flower that is shown here in an ancient Chinese scrolling vine pattern. The presence of a very traditional motif is often a feature of Nō costume design.
The small-scale checkered pattern in the background adds a certain richness to the appearance of this *asuita karaori*.
18th century.
Tokyo National Museum.

Page 112 :
A weave called *atsuita karaori* was developed in Nishijin during the latter part of the 17th century. It combined elements of the two fabrics after which it was named. As a Nō costume, the *atsuita karaori* could be used in roles served by either the *atsuita* or the *karaori* robe. In time it became indistinct as a robe type, and is no longer used in the present-day theater.

In Japan the cherry blossom has always been the most important of the spring flowers. Its short life evokes a melancholy sentiment. Here, the sadness is magnified by the drooping blossoms of the so-called "weeping" cherry tree.

The fancifully colored birds are carefully woven to appear as if they are in flight.

18th century.

Tokyo National Museum.

Page 113 (detail) :
Several kinds of leaves have served as autumnal motifs in Japanese art, the best-known being the maple leaf. Apart from being a symbol of fall, the leaf of the paper mulberry tree (so named because the tree's bark was used for making paper) was also employed as a unique surface upon which poetry was written in medieval times.

The leaves are very large in scale and appear with a geometric pattern imaginatively called "cypress wood fence."

18th century.

Tokyo National Museum.

The *chōken* is a costume type
that was developed for the Nō
stage. Its unlined gauze-weave
fabric and unstitched body
panels allowed the costume to
move gracefully during dance
movements.

The long-tailed birds hovering
over the bush clover were one of
several Japanese versions of the
auspicious Chinese creature
that is imprecisely called a
phoenix in the West.

Costumes in the *ōsode* category
were always worn as outer
robes, as were the medieval
garments upon which they were
modelled. When made of fabric
in a gauze weave, they provided
a subtle, veiled view of the costume worn underneath as an
inner robe.

18th century.

Tokyo National Museum.

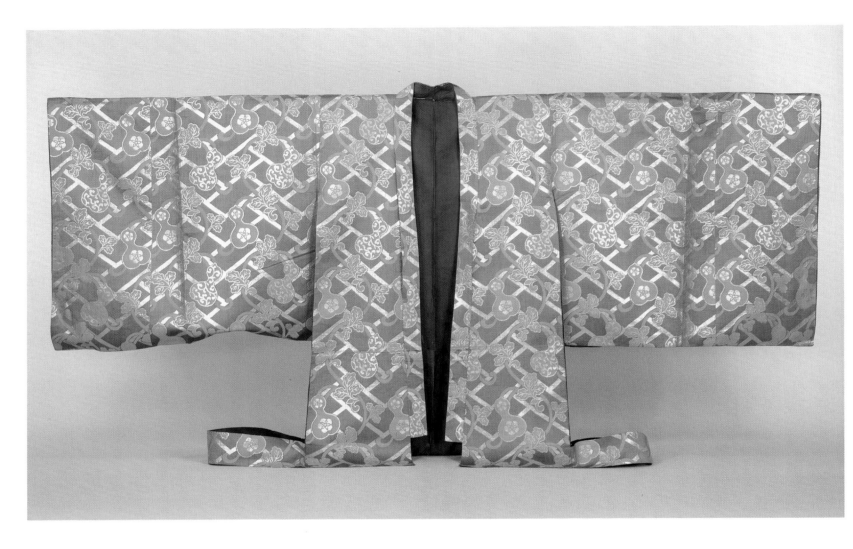

Above :
At the time this garment was made, the gourd was a popular motif that appeared on everyday clothing, and was appreciated for its playful shape. It is an unusual choice for the central motif of a Nō costume, especially one in the *ōsode* category.

The *happi* was used in both lined and unlined versions, primarily to represent armor worn by medieval military leaders. In this example the gourds are shown on vines and each gourd is internally patterned with either classical stylized flowers or scrolling tendrils. The addition of ancient motifs within the gourds was undoubtedly intended to give a more serious air to what then a popular image.
18th century.
Tokyo National Museum.

Page 117 :
The costume shaped like a sleeveless *happi* is known as the *sobatsugi*. It was worn by supporting characters of lower rank who were usually soldiers. Two of the gilded motifs in the polychrome and undyed squares are part of the set of myriad treasures. The other two motifs are the *rimbō*, a spikey wheel symbolizing the Buddhist law, and the *umban*, another Buddhist symbol (most prominent on the blue square at the center of the costume). Whereas the treasure symbols were popular motifs, the Buddhist symbols would have been too religious for general usage, such as on a *kosode*. However, the Buddhist emphasis on the transient nature of human existence was a recurring theme in Nō plays, and therefore Buddhist symbols were appropriate for a Nō costume.
18th century.
Tokyo National Museum.

Peonies framed by cloves appear in a composition that brings to mind Art Nouveau design of the following century. The cloves are arranged in the classical wavy line pattern and appear more ornate than usual, as do the peonies in the alternate horizontal rows of the design.

The *maiginu* costume was also intended primarily as a danse costume. When in motion, it moved more solemnly than the *chōken*. Its woven patterns are denser, resulting in a stiffer fabric, and the body panels were sewn along the sides, which further restricted the robe's movements.

18th century.

Tokyo National Museum.

(Detail) see back cover.

An *atsuita karaori* with the flower cart theme is shown against a lattice-work pattern. The carts are filled with a selection of *akikusa* and the ubiquitous fall flower, the chrysanthemum.

The position of every other cart is reversed in the pattern repeat and the color schemes and background coloration are varied. The changing color ground and lattice pattern give the motifs in this costume a greater sense of depth than those seen in the previous *nuihaku* costume (see page 96). The latter appear flat in their uniformly gilded and unpatterned surface.

These kinds of special effects liven up a woven repeat and show the skill of a creative designer.

18th century.

Tokyo National Museum.

Kesa,
The Essential
Buddhist Garment

INTRODUCTION

The garment that is the most typical and significant part of Buddhist dress is known as the *kesa*. As with *kosode* and Nō *shōzoku*, it is rectilinear in its outer shape and non-sculptural, in that its construction does not imitate the human form. The broad, flat, and usually rectangular-shaped *kesa* presents an ideal 'canvas' free of the constraints that forms place on surface design.

The *kesa* has essentially remained unchanged since its beginnings in the early centuries of Japanese Buddhism dating from the sixth century. Its history outside Japan stretches back to the sixth century B.C., in India, where the prince who became Buddha (literally the "Enlightened One") lived. In spite of its ancient past and sacred nature, *kesa* exhibit the opulence of materials, technical proficiency and creativity in design seen in *kosode* and Nō *shōzoku*. To understand the evolution of this garment, it is necessary to start with the beginnings of Buddhism.

THE EARLY HISTORY OF *KESA*

Accounts of Buddha's life and teachings were preserved as part of oral tradition during Buddhism's early centuries in India. As Buddhism spread to countries to the north and east of India, probably beginning in the 1st century A.D., written texts were compiled. The Chinese were the most diligent in the recording of Buddhist literature, and these records served as the primary source of Buddhist learning for the Japanese.

The origin of the word *kesa* can be found in the texts relating to the life of Buddha. During his early years as a prince, Buddha led a privileged and sheltered life. His chance encounters with poverty, sickness and death,

Above :
One of nine *kesa* belonging to Emperor Shōmu (701-756) which were donated to Tōdai-ji (*ji* means temple) upon his death. As Emperor, he established Buddhism as the national religion; and he became a Buddhist cleric when he abdicated in 749.
This *kesa* is somewhat in the *funzō-e* tradition, having been made of small, irregular-shaped scraps of cloth that are stitched together. It departs from strict ascetic garb in that the scraps are silk, brightly colored, organized into a columnar format, and most probably not made from discarded and soiled cloth.
8th century.
Collection of Shōsō-in, Nara.
Photo courtesy of the office of the Shōsō-in Treasure House.

Pages 120-121 :
The changing background is the result of ikat dyeing of the warps, and was a technique sometimes used in *karaori* Nō robes, especially in combination with long floating wefts and *kinran*, as in this example. The fabric employed here was not cut up into individual pieces and sewn together. Instead, lengths of the fabric were sewn side to side, and a purple silk cord was laid out to represent the traditional divisions of a *kesa*, and then sewn to the surface of the fabric. This cord overlay method represents a later stage in the development of *kesa*.
First half of the 19th century.
Private collection.
Photo courtesy of Jeffrey R. Hayden.

disturbed him and led to his quitting the palace in search of the meaning of human existence. In the first stage of his search for enlightenment, he lived as an ascetic, wearing *kashāya*-colored robes. *Kashāya* is a Sanskrit word which, when applied to color, refers to mixed, neutral or earth tones ; it also has connotations of impurity and uncleanliness. Later, on the path to enlightenment and during his life as Buddha, the texts relate that he wore a variety of clothing ranging from humble to fine.

The Chinese transliteration of *kashāya* became the word for the principal garment of the Buddhist clergy. The Japanese, in turn, transliterated the Chinese term, which resulted in the word *kesa*. The use of a word with lowly associations would seem to imply that the early forms of this garment were modelled after those worn by impoverished ascetics. This is partly borne out by the earliest extant *kesa*, all of which are preserved in Japan. Nine examples are documented as dating from the eighth century. Several other *kesa* are thought to have been in use during the seventh, eighth or ninth centuries. All early *kesa* are associated with important Indian, Chinese and Japanese Buddhist figures.

Many of these *kesa* can be classified as *funzō-e* (literally "robe made of excrement"). That is the term used for *kesa* made from small scraps of cloth stitched together. According to Buddhist texts, soiled and discarded scraps were most appropriate for the making of *funzō-e*. However, most of the early *funzō-e kesa* are attractively composed of colorful silk scraps which, given their great age and judging from their relative cleanliness, were not likely to have been collected from waste heaps. Although the scraps are randomly sewn, they are generally organized into columns and surrounded by a border. Two of the early *kesa*, which appear to be *funzō-e* are actually tapestry-woven imitations of the stitched *funzō-e*. They and

Side view illustrating the wearing of a *kesa*. Here, the *kesa* is worn covering both shoulders and over another garment. The manner of wearing *kesa* varies according to the sect of the wearer and the occasion.
10 ½ × 7 ½ in. (26.7 × 19.1 cm).
Zuzō Shuchi (1806).
Private collection.

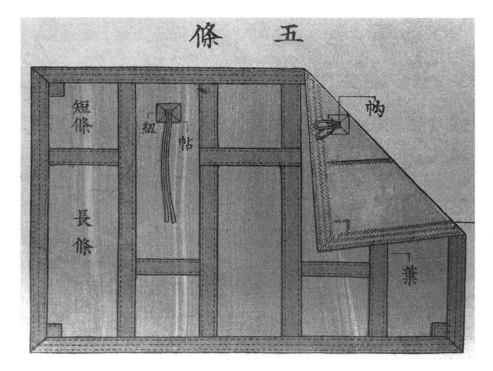

Page from a manual on *kesa* published for Buddhist clerics. The five-column *kesa* (*anda-e*) is illustrated and described as having columns of one long and one short section separated by a horizontal dividing strip. A border and vertical dividing strips delineate the columns. The corner squares and inner squares (one of each is unseen because a corner of the *kesa* is shown folded over) are also a regular feature of *kesa*.
The five-column *kesa* is used for everyday informal wear.
10 ½ × 7 ½ in. (26.7 × 19.1 cm).
Zuzō Shuchi (1806).
Private collection.

other early *kesa* that are not of the *funzō-e* type, are made of whole sections of cloth organized in the columnar format.

The degree to which these *kesa* depart from ragged and filthy dress is an indication of the various interpretations of Buddhism during its early history in India and, later, in China and Japan. Different sects quickly developed among the followers of Buddha in India, many of whom undoubtedly were influenced by their previous religious practices. Those who lived as ascetics would have probably continued to dress accordingly. Buddha probably realized that those of his followers who were more worldly and who did not lead hermitic lives, needed a distinctive garment as an outward symbol of their faith. Buddhist texts relate that he instructed a disciple to design a garment based on the ordered rows of plants in a rice field. This is thought to be the reason for the columnar format of *kesa*. This kind of garment gave a more formal appearance to those who became clergy in the organized sects of the religion. Later on, variations developed in the *kesa* which served to distinquish the clergy of different sects. The *kesa* also symbolized Buddhist learning, and its physical transmission from teacher to disciple became an important event in the propagation of the faith. Lay followers of Buddhism played a role by donating the cloth from which the *kesa* was made. In doing so, they would earn merit and provide their clergy with a garment that was more respectable than one made of dirty rags.

The early *funzō-e kesa* in Japan represent both the ascetic and organized tendencies of Indian Buddhism. Other early *kesa* and those of later periods exhibit further refinements in format and construction that were probably adaptations made outside India. *Kesa* were classified into three general categories according to the number of columns that were created by the placing of vertical dividing strips of cloth extending from the upper to the lower borders. Each column was internally divided by one or more horizontal strips, depending on the total number of columns in the *kesa*. *Kesa* of five columns are called *anda-e*, seven-columned *kesa* are called *uttarasō* and those with nine to twenty-five columns (but always an odd number, resulting in nine different possible numbers of columns) are termed *sōgyari*. The nine different columnar counts of the *sōgyari* were based on a system of rank modelled after a traditional nine-grade hierarchical Chinese law, with the greater number of columns corresponding to a higher rank.

The elaboration of *kesa* into the three different categories was another adaptation that probably occurred outside India. Buddhist texts recommended that clerics possess only three garments which, in traditional Indian dress, corresponded to a waist wrap, a covering for the upper body and a shawl worn over the torso. In countries like China and Japan, where the climate was colder, this minimal wardrobe was impractical. Instead, clerics wore their native dress according to the seasons, and wore either an *anda-e*, *sōgyari* or *uttarasō kesa* (depending on the occasion) wrapped toga-like over the left shoulder as an outer wear accessory. The Japanese names for the three categories of *kesa* were based on the Sanskrit terms for the three articles of dress originally specified in the texts, perhaps as a token of compliance with the three-garment rule.

Various methods of construction other than those used for the *funzō-e*, are evident in some of the early *kesa* and are more commonly seen in garments of later periods. Buddhist texts mention alternatives to *funzō-e* in deference to organized sects ; however, *kesa* made of uncut cloth are mentioned unfavorably. And for this reason, the two early tapestry-woven *kesa* would have been considered less proper, despite their visual resemblance to *funzō-e* and the presence of dividing strips sewn onto the fabric of the *kesa* in accordance with the "rice field" design. One variation of the above-mentioned method consisted of sewing only one edge of the dividing strips to an uncut cloth. This mode was probably considered more appropriate for *kesa*, since when this garment was worn the partially attached strips swayed, giving the impression of tattered clothing. This type of construction is rarely, if ever, seen in Japanese *kesa*. The methods most often encountered in Japanese *kesa* consisted of a sewn patchwork comprised of separate pieces of cloth for the borders, dividing strips and columns of the *kesa* ; and folded, stitched and overlapped sections of cloth which followed the "rice field" format.

Further modifications that probably occurred outside India include the addition of four square pieces of cloth at the four corners of the *kesa* within the borders. Another standard feature of the garment are two larger squares of cloth, on either side of the center column, just below the top border. Ties and straps were also sometimes attached for convenience. For more casual, everyday wear, abbreviated versions of the five-column *kesa* were developed and worn attached to a halter draped around the neck. As was the case in India, minor details of the kesa varied from sect to sect, according to Buddhist texts.

RITUALISTIC AND SYMBOLIC ASPECTS OF *KESA*

Before looking at the further evolution, of *kesa* in Japan, it is useful to note some of its ritualistic and symbolic aspects, in order to illustrate the religious significance of the garment, which remains relevant to Buddhists today. *Kesa* were meant to be sewn in a meditative way using specific kinds of stitches. The act of sewing a *kesa*, like the copying of Buddhist scriptures, was considered a devotional pursuit, and could be done either by clerics or laity. An important part of the ordination ceremony for a Buddhist cleric was the receiving of a *kesa*, which symbolized Buddhist teachings.

Prayers, such as the following, were uttered prior to putting on the *kesa*.
"How wondrous this deliverance robe is,
Like a field bestowing unlimited happiness !
Now we unfold the Buddha's teachings,
Making a vow to save all creatures."[1]

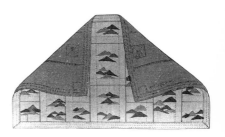

A seven-column *kesa* (*sōgyari*) with a tōyama ("distant mountain") pattern is depicted here. Each column is divided into the two long and one short section that is typical of the seven-column *kesa*.
10 ½ × 7 ½ in. (26.7 × 19.1 cm).
Zuzō Schuchi (1806).
Private collection.

Left :
Detail of a twenty-five column *kesa* worn by Kōgetsu Sōgan (1574-1643), who was the son of a wealthy merchant. The twenty-five column *kesa* was reserved for the highest ranking clerics such as Sōgan, the former abbot of Daitoku-ji.
This *kesa* was imported from China, as were many elaborate *kesa* prior to the 17th century. It was passed down to Sōgan from his teacher, as was the custom. *Kesa* were considered to be the embodiment of Buddhist learning.
Kinran was used extensively, as seen in the floral arabesques of the border and dividing strips. The columns feature a single, repeated sacred Sanskrit character that symbolizes a Buddhist deity ; and the corner squares display the Buddhist swastika. The character and the swastika are also rendered in *kinran*.
The construction of the *kesa* is unusual for its time because the border, dividing strips, columns and corner squares are not separate pieces of cloth that have been stitched together. Instead, the *kesa* is made from whole cloth that is woven to represent the traditional divided format of a *kesa*.
15th century.
Collection of Ryōkō-in, Kyoto.
Photo courtesy of Kyoto National Museum.

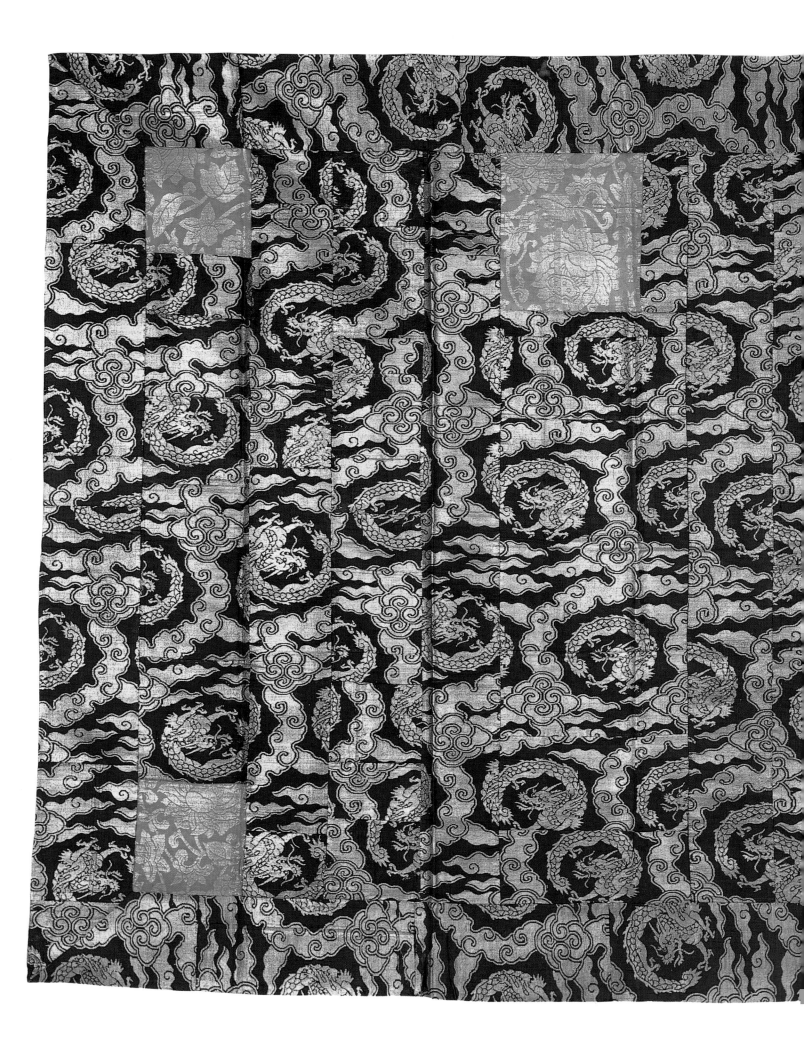

To insure that the *kesa* was treated with honor and respect, special procedures were followed for the wearing, cleaning, removing and folding of the garment.

The *kesa* itself can be considered as a mandala, a Sanskrit term for a symbolic rendering of the universe. The four corner squares represent the four cardinal directions, the center column symbolizes the Buddha, and the two flanking squares are his attendants.

JAPANESE BUDDHISM AND *KESA* OF THE MEDIEVAL AND *SENGOKU* PERIODS

D uring the medieval and *sengoku* periods, Buddhism continued to be important in Japanese life, both in a spiritual and a temporal way. Buddhism received extensive support from the court upon its introduction into Japan, where it was perceived as a meaningful vehicle for the importation of advanced foreign learning into the then illiterate and backwards Japan. Emperors also functioned as Buddhist leaders and allocated resources for the building of a network of temples and the creation of enormous quantities of Buddhist artifacts. Temples eventually controlled vast amounts of lands and formed their *own* armies of *sōhei* (warrior clerics) to protect their political and economic power. The Buddhist establishment proved to be a threat to the rule of the court, and later, to the samurai government which supplanted court rule late in the twelfth century.

Spiritually, Buddhism remained vital with the introduction of new Buddhist sects from China and the creation of new native sects. *Kesa*, as a symbol of learning that included the new teachings from abroad, continued to be brought into Japan. Dōgen (1200-53), who established the Sōtō branch of the Zen sect in Japan, was given the *kesa* of a Chinese Zen patriarch who had lived a century earlier. It had previously been passed down to Dōgen's teacher in China. Dōgen also wrote extensively on the subject of *kesa*, extolling its holy virtues and providing practical information concerning the making, care and use of the garment.

Extant *kesa* from the medieval and *sengoku* periods are generally quite opulent in materials, textile techniques and designs, especially when compared to the early *kesa*. Many of the *kesa* were made in China of fabrics not previously known in Japan, where they undoubtedly influenced the native textile industry. Included among the textile techniques found in surviving examples are a variety of embroidery stitches, weave techniques and the direct application of metallic leaf onto the fabric. Silk is the fiber used most exclusively, and gold and silver leaf are abundant. Motifs not traditionally associated with Buddhism, such as floral arabesques, floral sprays, dragons and phoenixes, are typical, as are motifs with specific religious symbolism, including the Buddhist treasure symbols and the ritual implement called the *vajra* in Sanskrit.

Pages 126-127 :
Dragon roundels and clouds in *kinran* create a striking effect against the dark blue background of this *kesa*. Because the parts of most *kesa* are cut from whole cloth, in accordance with Buddhist tradition, and then rearranged and sewn together as a patchwork, the repeat patterns that are inherent in woven fabrics become irregular and random in appearance in the finished *kesa*. The corner and inner squares, with a lotus arabesque in *kinran* on an orange ground, add another element of contrast to this *kesa*.
17th century.
Private collection.
Photo courtesy of Jeffery R. Hayden.

The extensive use of luxury fabrics and the presence of both Buddhist and non-Buddhist figural motifs, arrayed in elaborate patterns, represents a clear departure from the early *kesa*. The influence of Chinese Buddhism could account for the use of these fancy *kesa*, as China continued to be the mecca for Japanese Buddhists. It was probably this influence, along with the obvious presence of Chinese *kesa* in Japanese temples, and the desire of clerics to dress as befitted their positions of power, that led to the wearing of such expensive *kesa* in Japan.

The materialistic behavior of clerics was subject to criticism, as is seen in the following passage from the *Shōbō-genzō Zuimonki* by Dōgen.

"It is an obvious fact that Buddhism is now on the decline. I witnessed the gradual changes that had taken place between the first time I resided at Kennin-ji [*ji* means temple] and the time I returned there seven or eight years later. At the time every room of the temple was furnished with a lacquered case, and every monk had his own furniture, liked fine clothes, and stored away treasures. Not only that, but they loved to utter licentious words, neglecting the correct manner of salutation and worship."[2]

However, it is not certain that Dōgen would have disapproved of fancy *kesa*. In his essay entitled "Kesa Kudoku", which is a part of his major work, *Shōbō-genzō*, Dōgen shows a very practical-minded approach in discussing what fabrics should be used for making *kesa*, as he interprets from earlier Buddhist texts,

"A *kasāya* [*kesa*] should be made of coarse cotton cloth. When this is not available, fine cotton cloth should be used. When neither of the preceding is available, plain silk cloth may be used. When neither silk nor cotton cloth is available, light figured silk cloth may be used."[3]

BUDDHISM AFTER THE *SENGOKU* PERIOD

One of the major obstacles faced by Oda Nobunaga, the first of the great unifiers of the sixteenth century, was the power of the Buddhist establishment. In order to help consolidate his own landholdings and neutralize a potential military threat, certain temple strongholds were attacked. Mount Hiei, the seat of the Tendai sect, was ruthlessly destroyed in 1571. Hongan-ji, an important temple in Kyoto, was subdued as part of Nobunaga's successful attempt to control Kyoto. Hideyoshi continued the campaign against Buddhist power, suppressing the Mount Koya temple complex, where the headquarters of the Shingon sect was located. Tokugawa Ieyasu gained the final victory over the Buddhist establishment by the time he completed the unification of Japan in 1615.

Under Tokugawa rule, Buddhism became a part of the vast bureaucracy that was set up to control every aspect of life in Japan. Clerics were organized by region, sect and rank ; and the government created the post of Commissioner for Shrines and Temples. Every household was required

Detail of a portrait of Seigan Sōi (1586-1661), who was an abbot of the important Zen temple, Daitoku-ji, and later became abbot of a temple in Edo at the request of the shogun.
His *kesa* is elaborately patterned with a grapevine, which was a popular motif in Japanese art during the 16th and 17th centuries.
48 ¼ × 21 ¾ in. (122.6 × 55.3).
Collection of Kōtō-in, Kyoto.
Reproduced from *Daitoku-ji no meihō* (Treasures of Daitoku-ji), Kyoto National Museum, 1985, p.71.

This photograph of a Buddhist cleric was taken during the time when Japan was modernizing and Buddhism was in decline. *Kesa* were among the valuables that had to be sold by the once wealthy Buddhist temples.
His elaborate *kesa* has a design of fans, cranes and dragons.
10 ¾ × 8 ⅜ in. (27.3 × 21.5 cm).
Latter half of the 19th century.
Private collection.

to register at their local temple, where births, marriages and deaths were recorded. A great many temples were built to facilitate this form of local control. Under the registration system, everyone was considered to be a member of a Buddhist temple, regardless of their religious belief. Spiritually, it was a stagnant time for Buddhism in Japan. However, clerics benefitted materially from the support of the shogunate and from public donations that were sometimes demanded, for the performance of official and religious duties.

A loss of autonomy was the price paid for the comfortable position that clerics enjoyed under Tokugawa rule. An incident that clearly illustrates the government's control over religious matters was the so-called "purple *kesa*" controversy. For centuries, emperors had bestowed purple *kesa* upon the abbots of important temples. The shogunate's attempts to outlaw this

Sculpture of Ishin Sūden (1569-1632), a Zen Buddhist cleric, who was also a political power in the Tokugawa government. He is shown wearing a *kesa* with a cloud pattern in the dividing strips and chrysanthemums in the columns.

The *kesa* is worn in the standard way, draped diagonally over the left shoulder, where it is fastened by means of ties secured to a ring. A robe patterned with dragons can be seen underneath the *kesa*.

12 ⅞ in. (32.7 cm).

Collection of Nanzen-ji, Kyoto.
Photo courtesy of the Agency for Cultural Affairs, Tokyo.

practice were ignored. As punishment for their disobedience, the purple *kesa* of many abbots were revoked. In protest, Emperor Gomizuno-o abdicated in 1629, and clerics who voiced their dissent were banished.

Although the Buddhist establishment was no longer an independent force, its material well-being was secure through the Tokugawa rule. Ample funds were available for fine *kesa*, and the sumptuary laws, which mentioned Buddhist dress, apparently had little effect in regulating extravagance in *kesa*. With the demise of the shogunate in 1867 and the lessening of interest in traditional ways resulting from westernization, clerics faced a considerable loss in both government and public support. Many temples were forced to sell off possessions in order to meet expenses. As a result, large collections of Japanese Buddhist artifacts, including *kesa*, exist outside Japan.

KESA AFTER THE *SENGOKU* PERIOD

Luxurious *kesa* were made throughout the period of unification and the Tokugawa rule. The repertory of motifs and the variety of fabrics and techniques used in the making of *kesa* increased, allowing for greater diversity in the appearance of *kesa*. A tendency towards pictorialism developed, along with minimal adherence to the traditional divided "rice field" format. Also, the recycling of secular garments became more commonplace.

The majority of *kesa* were still being made of woven fabrics,but the cloth was likely to be a Nishijin product, as was true for Nō costumes, rather than an imported textile. Compound weaves including *kinran* and *ginran* are most commonly found among extant examples. Weaves as complex as *karaori*, employed in making the Nō robe of the same name, were also used for *kesa*.

The donation of secular garments, such as *kosode*, increased, as did the number of temples and the obligation of the public to provide 'compensation' for the duties performed by the clerics. Fabric from donated clothing was recycled into *kesa*, used for their linings and employed in the making of altar cloths and furnishing textiles for temples. Such donations were made by families in memory of a deceased person, by a lay person intending to become a cleric, or in the ancient tradition of the laity providing cloth for the making of *kesa*. Consequently, the luxuriousness of *kosode* was transferred in a very direct way to *kesa*.

A tradition of stitched *funzō-e* continued, but compared to early examples, the *kesa* of this type are sumptuous in appearance. In the later *funzō-e*-type *kesa*, the columns are made of irregularly shaped pieces of silk stitched together, but the borders, dividing strips, corner and inner squares

(Detail)
Later versions of the *funzō-e* style of *kesa* became less abstract in appearance and often incorporated fine weave patterned fabrics for parts of the *kesa* other than columns. These *kesa* became known as *tōyama* because the arrangement of small pieces of cloth suggested mountains ranges.
In this example, polychrome silk fragments in plain weave have been pasted and stitched together onto a while silk background. For the other parts of the *kesa* rich fabric, decorated with an ancient pattern of connecting hexagons and squares complements the curvilinear stitched fragments.
18th century.
Neutrogena Corporation Collection.

The design motifs of most *kesa* were drawn from the traditional repertory of Chinese symbols which were widely used in Japanese art from early times. These included dragons, clouds, and flowers, both real, such as the lotus, peony and chrysanthemum, and imaginary. Variations in the scale, coloration, juxtaposition and materials used to render the motifs produced interesting designs and greatly expanded the visual possibilities of a limited range of symbols.
Four different patterns are seen in the fabrics used for this *kesa* : large-scale peonies and leaves, imaginary flowers on a diaper of Y-shaped elements, dragon roundels and clouds, and for the border and dividing strips, an arabesque featuring paulownias.
17th century.
Stephen Gomez Collection.
Photo courtesy of Jeffrey R. Hayden.

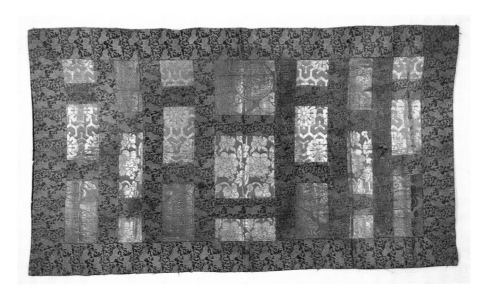

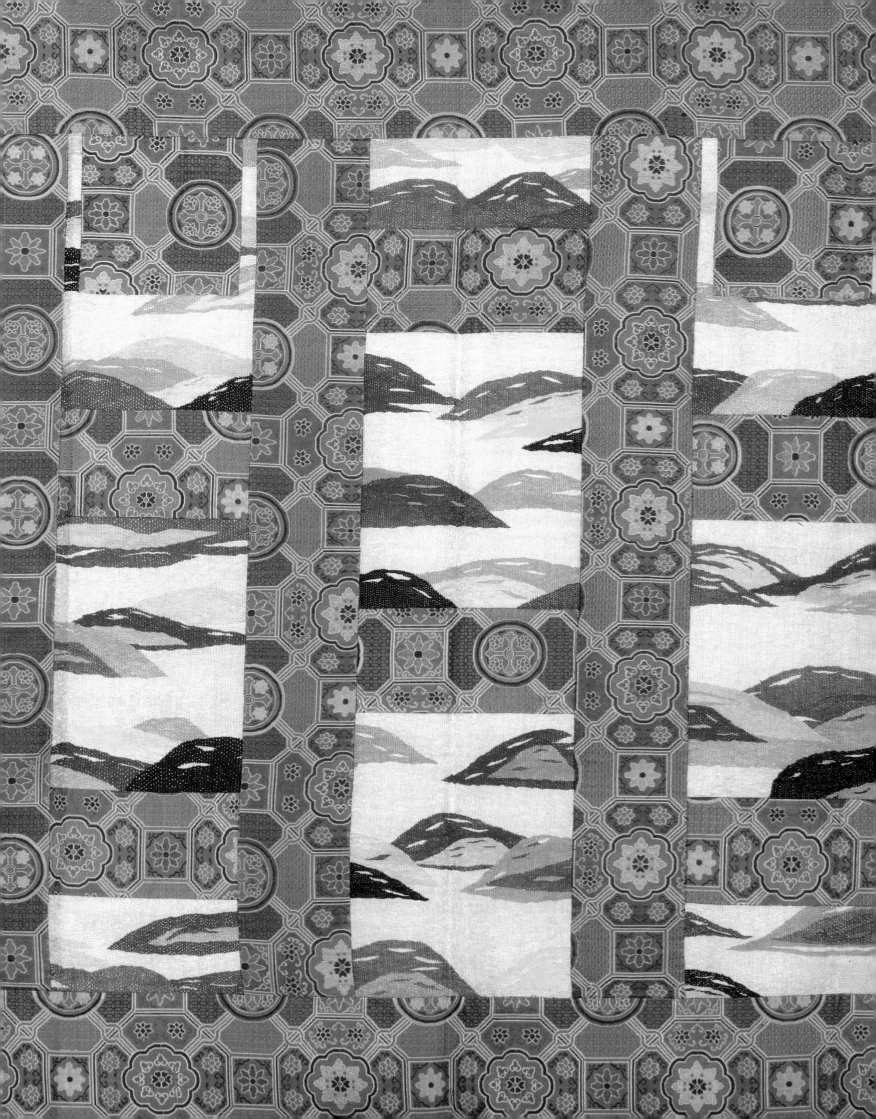

are usually made of an expensive compound-weave fabric. Furthermore, a tendency developed to avoid random arrangement of the silk pieces. Instead, an attempt was made to create the appearance of distant mountain ranges (*tōyama*) in the assembly and sewing together of the bits of silk. These *kesa* were called *tōyama* in recognition of their pictorial intent, and possibly as an alternative to the use of the word *funzō*, which had unpleasant connotations.

Pictorialism is also seen in the creation of complete scenes featuring subjects as diverse as mythical creatures, landscapes, musical instruments, flower baskets and assemblies of legendary sages. Techniques including tapestry weave, compound weaves, embroidery and *yūzen* were employed to render the scenes. Usually, thin cording made of gilt threads was stitched onto these *kesa* in token respect for the "rice field" tradition. Less commonly, the dividing lines were woven into the design of the fabric, drawn onto the face of the cloth, or created by folds which were sewn down to keep them in place. In the most costly examples, the weaving of individual parts of a *kesa* was carefully planned and executed in order to create a perfectly matched, continuous design when the assembled parts were sewn together.

As in medieval times, there was criticism of extravagance among clerics, including their dress. Sontaku Ninomiya (1787-1856), a noted religious philosopher, contrasted the behavior of clerics in his time with the ways of early Buddhists.

"Ancient priests took their own bowls and obtained their own living by begging. They dressed in mean clothes and were content to live in mountain caves or in the quiet of the forest. But modern priests live in luxury, dress in costly robes and sit proudly in their magnificent temples, acting contrary to all the teachings of Buddha."[4]

Kūkai (744-835), one of the founders of Japanese Buddhism, would have had a more compassionate view than Ninomiya. He preached that enlightenment was the goal of Buddhist teachings, not the suppression of human desire. Those who achieved enlightenment moved beyond the conflicts inherent in life.

NOTES

1. Yūhō Yokoi, *Zen Master Dōgen : An Introduction With Selected Writings*, New York, John Weatherhill, Inc., 1976, p. 102.

2. Ibid., p. 33.

3. Ibid., p. 99.

4. Robert Armstrong, *Buddhism and Buddhists in Japan*, New York, The Macmillan Co., 1927, p. 23.

Plates

Photograph of Buddhist monks illustrating the manner of wearing *kesa*. The cleric on the right is wearing a *kesa* around his mid-section which is supported by a single strap over his left shoulder.
The other cleric is wearing his *kesa* draped over his left shoulder.
Second half of 19th century.
Collection A.E.D.T.A., Paris.

A single motif, clouds, are depicted here, but in seemingly endless variation. The color schemes of the polychrome clouds change as identically-shaped clouds are repeated. In the corner and inner squares, the cloud image appears again, this time in *kinran*, and in a smaller scale than the polychrome clouds.

The dating of *kesa* is often the result of educated guesswork, especially in the absence of a temple record that would provide a provenance or a dated inscription on the lining of the garments. The traditional motifs were faithfully based on earlier models ; and textile materials and techniques that were most often used for *kesa* underwent little change. Chronology is often a matter of " feel " based on the way in which the textile has aged.

18th century.

Association for the Study and Documentation, of Asian Textiles (A.E.D.T.A.), Paris n° 1702.

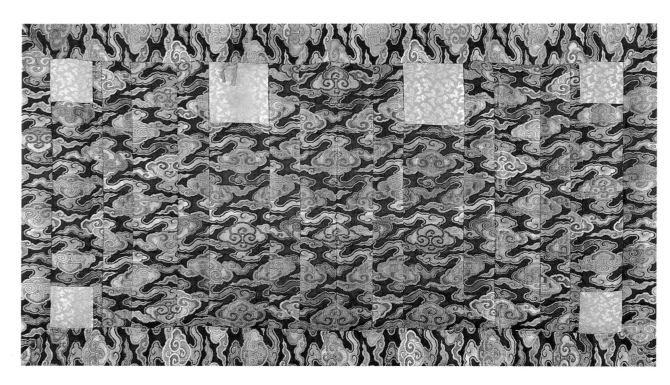

The ancient wavy line pattern, also seen in Nō robes, is ingeniously rendered here. Fan shapes, which are alternately flipped over and laid end to end, create an illusion of continuity in spite of the patchwork format of the *kesa*. Stylized flowers with petals facing in opposite directions fill the spaces in between the curves. Larger-scale flowers and a phoenix roundel appear on the corner and inner squares.

18th century.

Don Erickson Collection.
Photo courtesy of Jeffrey R. Hayden.

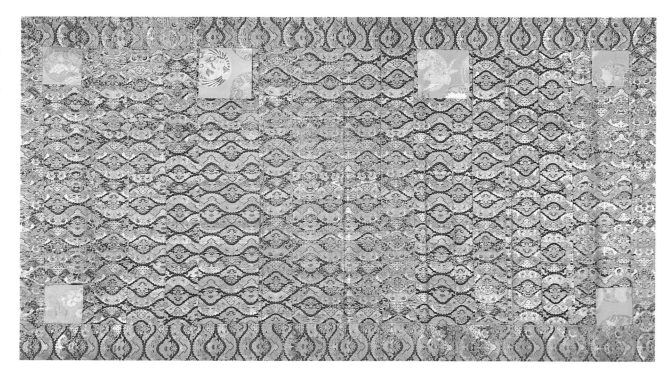

A diamond-shaped arrangement of an ancient stylized floral motif is repeated throughout this *kesa* producing quite a stimulating effect. The long floating wefts that are characteristic of the *karaori* weave randomly vary in color from diamond to diamond, breaking the monotony of the repeated motif. The cutting, rearranging and sewing of the pieces of cloth from which the *kesa* was made add futher spontaneity to the overall design.
17th century.
Private collection.
Photo courtesy of Jeffrey R. Hayden.

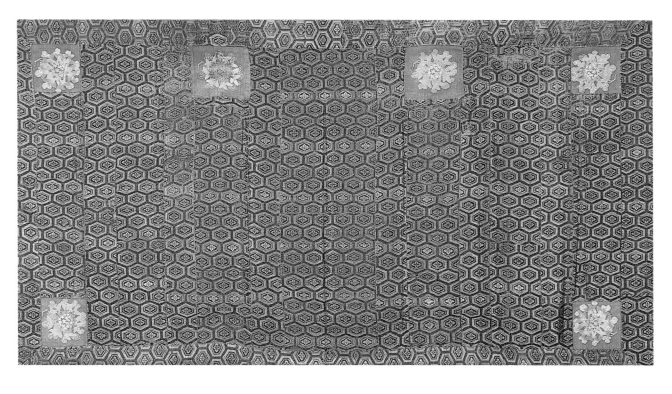

As in the previous example, a repeated motif woven with long floating wefts takes on a more interesting appearance when used in the *kesa* format, even though the color scheme of the fabric is more regular than in the other *kesa*. The corner and inner squares are prominent because they differ in color, weave and motif from the main fabric.
17th century.
Private collection.
Photo courtesy of Jeffrey R. Hayden.

Another example of a *kesa* made from fabric similar to that used for Nō costumes, in this instance one of the *atsuita* type. The lotus medallions appear to be suspended over the " cypress fence " pattern. *Kinran* is used abundantly here, as in *atsuita* Nō robes. The corner and inner squares show a checkered pattern containing floral motifs.
First half of the 19th century.
Private collection.
Photo courtesy of Jeffrey R. Hayden.

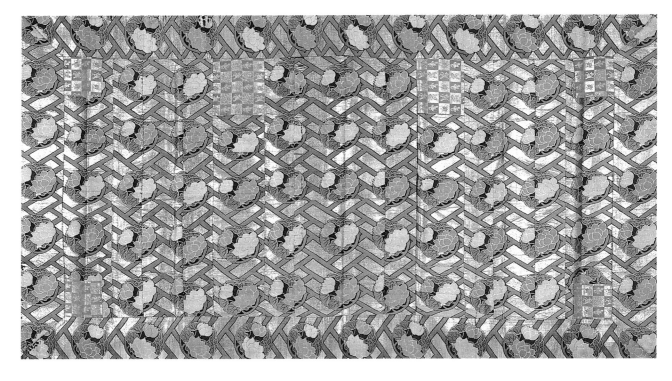

A creative but rarely seen alternative to the customary cut and sewn patchwork *kesa* was the *kesa* made from whole cloth woven with a patchwork pattern. Columns and dividing strips are not clearly defined in this example, but may have originally been denoted by cording sewn onto the face of the garment.
The coloration and patterning seen here was possibly influenced by *sarasa* (chintz), which is what the Japanese called the Indian printed and painted cottons that were widely admired. Examples of patchwork-design chintz have survived in Japan, as have Japanese-made imitations with a similar pattern, of which this *kesa* may have been a woven version.
Late 18th/early 19th century.
British Museum, London, courtesy of the trustees.

Photo courtesy of Jeffrey R. Hayden.

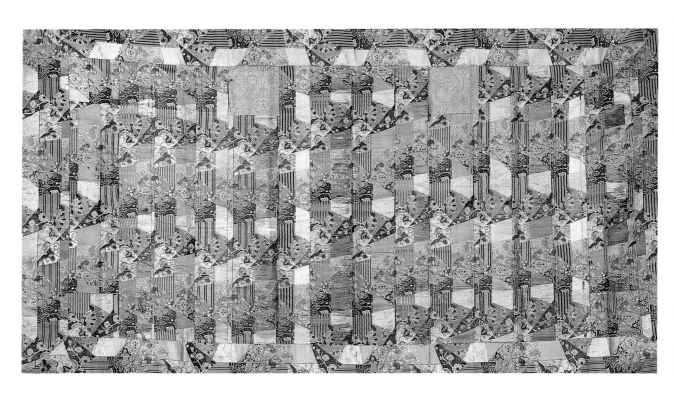

Three fabrics, each very different in appearance, but all making use of metallic paper strips, are used for the various parts of this *kesa*. The border and dividing strips have a checkered pattern showing treasure symbols in *ginran* and blue silk. A *kinran* fabric with mythical birds and stylized peonies serves as the corner and inner squares. Lastly, the columns have fanciful leaf and flower motifs that include some *ginran*.
Late 18th/early 19th century.
A.E.D.T.A., Paris.
Nº 1629.

Left (detail) :
Flowering peony branches and scattered characters alluding to a poem (visible on the top border) are the design elements in this *kosode* that was transformed into a *kesa*.
Kosode were given to temples for various reasons and were remade to serve primarily as furnishing fabrics and *kesa*. A widow, or a woman who disgraced her family might donate her finer garments upon joining a temple. The laity were expected to donate money and goods to temples, and luxury clothing was considered to be a suitable gift. More commonly, the better *kosode* of a deceased person were given to a temple in their memory.
Late 18th/early 19th century.
Private collection.
Photo courtesy of Jeffrey R. Hayden.

Right (detail) :
The embroidered pine, bamboo, plum, tortoise and crane motifs were a typical combination of images for a wedding robe. This former *kosode* might have belonged to a young widow who became a nun upon her husband's death, or perhaps it was given to a temple by a husband who lost a young wife.
Late 18th/early 19th century.
Private collection.
Photo courtesy of Jeffrey R. Hayden.

Left (detail) :
Stylized and naturalistic chrysanthemums appear to be super-imposed on the *kinran* wave motifs. This kind of design with a multi-layered visual effect and long weft floats, was also used for Nō robes of the *karaori* type.

18th century.

A.E.D.T.A., Paris.
N° 2136.

Left (detail) :
The use of similar kinds of luxury fabrics in the making of certain *kesa* and Nō costumes represents one of the parallels that *kesa* share with non-religious garments. An even closer association between sacred and secular costume resulted from the practice of remaking *kosode* into *kesa*.
A typical *katabira* type of *kosode* was cut up and reassembled to make this *kesa*. The edges of the *kosode* sections have overlapped, creating the appearance of vertical strips which serve to delineate the *kesa*'s columns. This visual effect results from the doubling of the translucent gauze *katabira* fabric.

18th century.

Konantz-Benton-Minnich Collection, Minnesota Museum of Art, Saint Paul.
Photograph courtesy of Minnesota Museum of Art, Saint Paul.

Pages 144-145 (details) :
This composition, which is unusual for a tapestry-woven *kesa*, consists of two large medallions containing auspicious symbols, including a bat, peach and fungus. The medallion format was common in textile design, but was not used in paintings.
Colorful clouds fill the background, adding to the otherworldly appearance of this *kesa*.
(see also pages 6-7)

First half of the 19th century.

A.E.D.T.A., Paris.
N° 2970.

Pictorial *kesa* were also executed in a kind of tapestry weave called *tsuzure-ori*. Adjacent weft threads in different colors do not interlock, resulting in motifs with sharp outlines. These *kesa* are generally woven on wide looms, and remain uncut, with cords sewn onto them to represent the traditional *kesa* divisions.

Here, a pair of phoenixes are shown in a landscape with flowers, birds, a stream, rocks and clouds. Such a scene would not be out of place as the subject of a screen painting. Only the presence of cords and corner and inner squares identify it as a *kesa* rather than a woven version of a painting.

First half of the 19th century.

Jon Eric Riis Collection.
Photo courtesy of Jeffrey R. Hayden.

In another scene that can easily be imagined as a screen painting, a pair of lion-like beasts are pictured in a traditional combination with peonies, and in a landscape setting. The presence of motifs with heavy black outlines is common in tapestry-woven *kesa*, and was based on a convention originally borrowed from Chinese painting.

Often, the threads dyed to produce a dark color such as black were also treated with an iron mordant in order to set the dye.

This can cause the deterioration of those threads over time, as has happened in this example, which was later restored.

First half of the 19th century.

Jon Eric Riis Collection.
Photo courtesy of Jeffrey R. Hayden.

Right (detail) :
Pictorial *kesa* became popular in the 18th and 19th centuries. These *kesa* are among the most costly and intricate examples ever made in Japan. At times, they exhibit compositions that are reminiscent of those seen in paintings.

Here, a variety of floral arrangements in baskets, vases and on a stand are shown interspersed with flowers and stylized floral medallions. Individual parts of the *kesa* were carefully woven in order to create a completed picture when assembled. Portions of images that appear on dividing strips, columns and corner and inner squares show up as full images in the *kesa*. A simpler method also used in the making of this and some other pictorial *kesa* involved folding and sewing to indicate separations between *kesa* parts. Motifs that span pieces of the garment usually appear slightly off register at a seam when this method is used. *Kesa* made in these ways stretched the visual boundaries of patchwork, while still adhering to the traditional pieced construction.
Late 18th/early 19th century.
Private collection.
Photo courtesy of Jeffrey R. Hayden.

Page 149 (detail) :
Pictorial *kesa* often depicted mythic themes, rather than realistic subject matter such as flower arranging and Bugaku. The phoenix was a composite mythological creature borrowed from Chinese art. It became a symbol of the empress in Japan.
Late 18th/early 19th century.
A.E.D.T.A., Paris.
No 1494.

This pictorial *kesa* contains motifs representing musical instruments, masks and a hat associated with Bugaku, an ancient music and dance form used in court and Buddhist rituals. One motif, a *gakubiwa* (a sort of lute), spans every possible *kesa* part : the border, a corner square, and two different columns and dividing strips. Extremely precise weaving successfully depicts a single motif that was spread across so many different costume parts.
Late 18th/early 19th century.
Lowie Museum of Anthropology, The University of California at Berkeley.

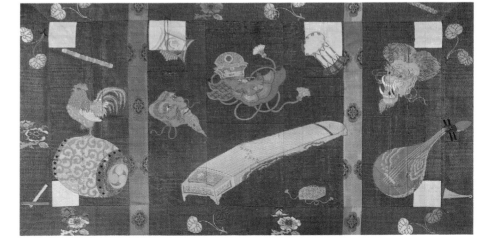

Pages 150-151 (detail) :
Kesa differ in details of construction according to the sect for which they were made. Some have narrow borders, and an inner square with a tie attached on both the front and the lining of the garment. Others are trapezoidal such as this example, (for technical reasons reproduced as a rectangle) which was probably worn by a cleric of the Jōdo sect or the Rinzai branch of the Zen sect. The white background provides a striking contrast to the polychrome peonies and clouds.
18th century.
A.E.D.T.A., Paris.
N° 1646.

Epilogue

I n Japan, more so than in other industrialized nations, traditional arts have not only endured, but they have flourished. The special attitudes that enable a people to infuse their past with vitality and current relevance have not always existed in modern Japan. At the time of rapid westernization, during the last third of the nineteenth century, many of the leading citizens eagerly mimicked foreign ways, often with comical results. Along with this behavior, there existed a sense of shame in regard to the 'quaint' ways of old Japan.

In a short time, Japan transformed itself from a feudal country with no rail transportation, rapid communication system, or viable military force into a modern state that was able to defeat Russia in a war early in this century. The remarkable success of the Japanese in emulating the expansionist policies of their western counterparts ultimately led to their downfall in World War II. They emerged from almost total devastation to build what is today the world's strongest economy.

The rejection of the past that was inherent in the modernization process proved to be a threat to Japan's cultural patrimony. The outflow of artistic treasures that took place was largely halted at the end of the nineteenth century with the creation of a government agency that registered and protected works of art. Since that time, objects of all kinds, including costumes, have come to be designated as Important Cultural Properties and National Treasures.

With the passage of time came the realization that it was not only important to save the artifacts, but also the skills that were used to create them. The Living National Treasures were first designated in the mid-1950's. Among them are included several practitioners of textile techniques, such as *yūzen*, indigo dyeing and paste resist dyeing. Costumes that are made by these masters are sold for prices that are as high or even higher than those for contemporary painting and sculpture in Japan. These costumes follow the *kosode* shape and usually employ traditional motifs. Their designs are both beautiful and creative, proving that even with limited subject matter and a higly structured format, there can be endless possibilities for artistic potential.

Apart from the nationally recognized artisans whose work has continued the creativity of the *kosode* tradition, there are also workshops which faithfully reproduce historic costumes for utilitarian purposes. Nō theater and Buddhism are both very much alive in Japan today, and consequently there is still a demand for Nō costumes and *kesa*. Nō actors and Buddhist clerics still prefer garments made in traditional manner, even though they are quite costly.

Reproductions of *kosode* are also being produced today. Because the originals are so fragile, copies are used by museums and organizations for displays and exhibitions, and are occasionally worn by participants in films, festivals and weddings. Increased interest in traditional dress has led to the establishment of schools for kimono-wearing and obi-tying and has added to the demand for *kosode*-like garments.

As for the general population, the clothes that are worn on a daily basis are indistinguishable from those seen in European and American cities. However, the *yukata*, which is cut like the *kosode* and worn with a sash, is commonly used for casual wear in the Japanese home. The comfortable experience of wearing a *yukata* is also available to anyone staying in a Japanese hotel or inn. Along with towels and soap, all rooms are thoughtfully equipped with slippers and *yukata*.

In recent years, several Japanese designers, such as Issey Miyake, Yohji Yamamoto and Rei Kawakubo, have put Japan on the fashion map. Their work has received international acclaim, and yet it continues to reflect some of the sensibilities that stem from the rich heritage of Japanese dress. The clothes of these designers tend to be loose rather than form-fitting, generally non-specific as to gender, and highly sophisticated in terms of the fabrics that are employed. They are alluring reflections of a culture that manages to be both traditional and modern at the same time.

The *koshimaki*, a samurai-class *kosode* type, was quite limited in its motifs and design formats. Decoration usually consisted of small-scale auspicious motifs that were densely embroidered on dark *nerinuki* silk. The garment was worn off the shoulders, over an unlined summer robe such as a *katabira* or *hitoe*.

The *takara zukushi* (myriad treasures) are standard motifs on *koshimaki*. This set of symbols are predominantly Chinese in origin and include a pair of cloves (a Japanese misinterpretation of rhinoceros horns, which were a Chinese symbol of happiness), the key to a treasure chest, jewels, a money pouch and a magic hat, among others.

First half of the 19th century.

Tokyo National Museum.

Appendices

Glossary

anda-e : *kesa* of five columns.

atsuita : type of *Nō* costume usually worn for male roles.

atsuita karaori : type of *Nō* costume combining features of the *atsuita* and the *karaori Nō* costumes.

chirimen : a type of crepe cloth.

chayazome : dyeing process featuring indigo and involving the use of paste as a resist. Also the name for a *kosode* style employing this process.

chōnin : townspeople consisting of the merchant and artisan classes.

compound weave : technique for patterning fabric employing more than one warp or more than one weft, or both multiple warps and wefts.

daimyo : regional leaders of the samurai class.

edozuma : *kosode* style characterized by a balanced arrangement of design motifs.

furisode : type of *kosode* with long, dangling sleeves.

funzō-e : a way of making *kesa* involving the stitching together of small scraps of cloth.

Genroku : *kosode* style named after an era (1688-1704), but popular after the end date of that era.

ginran : thin strips of paper covered with silver foil.

goshodoki : *kosode* style favored by the upper class.

hiinagata bon : woodblock-printed books of *kosode* designs.

hitoe : type of unlined *kosode* worn in summer.

Kanbun : *kosode* style named after an era (1661-1673).

kanoko : spot motif produced by *shibori* or stencil dyeing.

karaori : a compound-weave fabric characterized by long, floating wefts. Also the name for

a type of *Nō* costume made of this sort of fabric.

kashāya : Sanskrit term from which the word *kesa* is derived.

katabira : type of unlined *kosode* made of ramie and worn in summer.

Keichō : *kosode* style named after an era (1596-1615), but popular beyond the end date of that era.

kesa : mantle worn by Buddhist clerics.

kinran : thin strips of paper covered with gold foil.

koshimaki : type of *kosode* worn as a summer over robe. Also the name for a way of wearing a garment off the shoulders and draping over the *obi*.

kosode : forerunner of the modern day kimono characterized by narrow openings for the hands at the sleeve ends. Also the name for a specific type of this garment, distinct from other types such as the *furisode, katabira, uchikake*, etc.

nerinuki : plain woven fabric with raw silk warp and degummed silk weft.

noshime : type of *Nō* costume that is relatively plain in design.

nuihaku : *kosode* style characterized by embroidery and metallic foil. Also the name for a type of *Nō* costume using the same techniques.

obi : sash for fastening the *kosode*.

onnagata : male actors who play female roles.

ōsode : general name for an old-style garment with wide sleeves unsewn at the ends.

pattern dyeing : process for patterning whole cloth involving the use of pastes, ties, stitches or clamps to prevent dye penetration in certain areas of a fabric. The ikat method of tie-dyeing threads prior to weaving them into fabric can be considered another method of pattern dyeing.

plain weave : technique for unpatterned fabric consisting of a single warp and a single weft,

with both warp and weft showing equally on the surface of the fabric.

rinzu : figured silk fabric in a satin weave.

sakoku : the official closing-off of Japan to the outside world, lasting from the 1630's to 1853.

sankin-kōtai : system requiring daimyo to spend alternate years in Edo, where their wives and children were forced to live permanently.

satin weave : technique for a patterned or unpatterned fabric in which the single warp and single weft combine, resulting in the unequal exposure of warp and weft in the ratio of four to one, or more, on the surface of the fabric.

sengoku : the period of civil war in Japan lasting from the 1460's to the 1560's.

shibori : method of pattern dyeing primarily involving stitching, tying or pinching off areas of fabric to prevent dye penetration.

shite : principal actor in a *Nō* play.

shōzoku : general name for costumes worn by actors in *Nō* theater performances.

sōgyari : *kesa* of nine to twenty-five columns.

surihaku : application of metallic foil to fabric. Also the name for a type of *Nō* costume made of this kind of fabric.

tapestry weave : technique in which the single warp is completely covered by the single weft which serves to give pattern to the fabric.

tsujigahana : *kosode* style characterized by *shibori* sometimes in combination with embroidery, metallic foil or ink painting.

uchikake : type of *kosode* worn cloak-like as an over robe.

ukiyo : term used for the hedonistic life of the pleasure quarter.

uttarasō : *kesa* of seven columns.

waki : supporting actor in a *Nō* play.

yūzen : *kosode* style combining the materials and techniques of both painting and dyeing.

Selected bibliography

ADDISS, Stephen, *The Art of Zen* New York, Abrams, 1989.

BETHE, Monica, PAUL, Margot and MAYER STINCHECUM, Amanda, *Kosode, 16th-19th Century Textiles from the Nomura Collection*, New York, Japan Society/Kodansha International, 1984.

Bunka Gakuen Costume Museum, *Meihen shō* (Treasures of the collection), Tokyo, 1979.

FEDDERSEN, Martin, *Japanese Decorative Art : A Handbook for Collectors and Connoisseurs*, trans. by Katherine Watson, New York, Thomas Yoseloff, 1962.

FISTER, Patricia, *Japanese Women Artists 1600-1900*, New York, Harper & Row, 1988.

GOODWIN, Shauna J. *The Shape of Chic : Fashion and Hairstyles in the Floating World*, New Haven, Yale University Art Gallery, 1986.

HAYES, Jr., Joseph S., HYOBU Nishimura, and MAILEY Jean, *Tagasode : Whose Sleeves... Kimono from the Kanebo Collection*, New York, Japan Society, 1976.

HENRY, Charles-Arsène, « Tapisseries et soieries japonaises », *Bulletin de la maison franco-japonaise*, vol. 12, nᵒ 1, Paris, Geuthner, 1941.

ISHIMURA, Hayao, MARUYAMA Nobuhiko, and YAMANOBE Tomoyuki, *Robes of Elegance : Japanese Kimonos of the 16th-20th centuries*, trans. by Haruko Ward, Raleigh, North Carolina Museum of Art, 1988.

ITŌ, Toshiko, *Tsujigahana : The Flower of Japanese Textile Art*, trans. by Monica Bethe, New York, Kodansha International, Ltd., 1981.

IZUTSU, Gafu, *Kesa shi* (History of *Kesa*), Tokyo, Yuzan Kaku, 1978.

IZUTSU, Gafu, *Hō-e shi* (History of religious garments), Tokyo, Yuzan Kaku, 1978.

Japan Society, *Autumn Grasses and Water : Motifs in Japanese Art*, New York, Japan Society, 1983.

Japan Textile Color Design Center, *Textile Designs of Japan, Volume I : Free-Style Designs, Volume II : Geometric Designs*, New York, Kodansha International, Ltd., 1980.

KEENE, Donald, *Nō : Classical Theater of Japan*, Tokyo, Kodansha, 1966.

KENNEDY, Alan, « Kesa : Its Sacred and Secular Aspects, » *The Textile Museum Journal*, vol.22, 1983.

KOMPARU, Kunio, *The Nō Theater : Principles and Perspectives*, trans. by Jane Corddry, New York, John Weatherhill, Inc., 1983.

Kyoto National Museum, *Daitokuji meiho* (Treasures of Daitoku-ji), Kyoto, Nihon Keizai Shimbun, Inc., 1985.

Kyoto National Museum, *Kyo no senshoku bi : Monoyama kara edo made* (Beauty of Kyoto textiles : Monoyama through Edo periods), Kyoto, Kyoto National Museum, 1975.

Kyoto National Museum, *Nihon no senshoku : gi to bi* (Japanese textiles : beauty and skill), Kyoto, Kyoto-Shoin, 1987.

LIDDELL, Jill, *The Story of the Kimono*, New York, E. P. Dutton, 1989.

LINK, Howard, *The Feminine Image : Women of Japan*, Honolulu, Honolulu Academy of Arts, 1985.

LYMAN, Marie, « Distant Mountains : The Influence of Funzō-e on the Tradition of Buddhist Clerical Robes in Japan, » *The Textile Museum Journal*, vol.23, 1984.

MINNICH, Helen Benton, *Japanese Costume and the Makers of Its Elegant Tradition*, Rutland, Vermont, Charles E. Tuttle Co., 1963.

MURASE, Miyeko, *Tales of Japan : Scrolls and Prints from The New York Public Library*, New York, Oxford University Press, 1986.

NAKAOKA, Tetsuro, et. al., « The Textile History of Nishijin (Kyoto) : East Meets West, » *Textile History*, vol.19, nᵒ 2, 1988.

NOMA, Seiroku, *Japanese Costume and Textile Arts*, trans. by Armins Nikovskis, New York, Weatherhill/Heibonsha, 1977.

Sakai City Museum, *Nui : kosode o irodoro* (Embroidery : decorative technique in *kosode*), Sakai, Sakai City Museum, 1987.

Seattle Art Museum, *A Thousand Cranes*, San Francisco, Seattle Art Museum/Chronicle Books, 1987.

SHIVELY, Donald, « Sumptuary Regulations and Status in Early Tokugawa Japan, » *Harvard Journal of Asiatic Studies*, vol.25, 1964-65.

Tokyo National Museum, *Tokubetsu tenkan : Nō Kyōgen Shōzoku* (Special exhibition of Nō

Index of costume styles and types

and Kyōgen costumes), Tokyo, Tokyo National Museum, 1987.

Tokyo National Museum, *Tokyo Kokuritsu Hakubutsukan zuhan mokuroku : kosode fukushoku hen* (Illustrated catalogues of the Tokyo National Museum : *Kosode* costume volume), Tokyo, Tokyo National Museum, 1983.

Tokyo National Museum, *Tokyo Kosuritsu Hakubutsukan zuhan mokuroku : Nō shoku hen* (Illustrated catalogues of the Tokyo National Museum : Nō costume volume), Tokyo, Tokyo National Museum, 1987.

WATSON, William, ed., *The Great Japan Exhibition : Art of the Edo Period 1600-1868*, London, Royal Academy of Arts/Weidenfeld and Nicolson, 1981.

YANG, Sunny and NARASIN Rochelle M., *Textile Art of Japan*, Tokyo, Shufunotomo Co., Ltd., 1989.

YOKOI, Yūhō, *Zen Master Dōgen : An Introduction with Selected Writings*, New York, John Weatherhill, Inc., 1976.

YOSHIDA, Mitsukuni, *The People's Culture from Kyoto to Edo*, trans. by Lynne E. Riggs, Tokyo, Mazda Motor Corp., 1986.

YOSHIOKA, Sachio, ed. *Senshoku no bi* (Textile art), « Yūzen, » n° 3, early Spring, 1980 ; « Nō shōzoku, » n° 4, Spring, 1980 ; « Furisode, » n° 15, early Spring, 1982 ; « Edo no kosode, » n° 21, early Spring, 1983.

Photography Credits